Contents

Introduction

We cherish our "Christmas things" for the memories they hold—an ornament made by someone special, a wreath to welcome friends, an heirloom crèche that tells a wondrous story. These symbols of the season bring joy and comfort year after year. As with old friends, we delight in seeing them again.

In *Quilted for Christmas, Book II*, you'll find a medley of festive quilts and wall hangings just waiting to become a part of your Christmas traditions.

Classic renditions of timeless patterns will please those who favor the traditional look, while original designs offer fresh interpretations of holiday themes. There are projects for every skill level and a variety of quiltmaking techniques.

As every quilter knows, it's never too early to begin a Christmas quilt! Choose your favorite project from this eclectic collection and gather the perfect fabrics. Then steal some time and start to stitch a new Christmas memory.

Quiltmaking Basics

FABRIC

Select high-quality, 100% cotton fabrics. They hold their shape well and are easy to handle. Cotton blends can be more difficult to stitch and press. Sometimes, however, a cotton blend is worth a little extra effort if it is the perfect fabric for your quilt.

Yardage requirements are provided for all the projects in this book and are based on 42" of usable fabric after preshrinking. Some quilts call for an assortment of scraps. If you have access to scraps, feel free to use them and purchase only those fabrics you need to complete the quilt you are making.

Preshrink all fabric to test for colorfastness and remove excess dye. Wash dark and light colors separately so that dark colors do not run onto light fabrics. Some fabrics may require several rinses to eliminate the excess dyes. Iron fabrics so that you can cut out the pieces accurately.

SUPPLIES

Sewing Machine: To machine piece, you'll need a sewing machine that has a good straight stitch. You'll also need a walking foot or darning foot if you are going to machine quilt.

Rotary-Cutting Tools: You will need a rotary cutter, cutting mat, and clear acrylic rulers in a variety of sizes, including 6" x 24" and 12" x 12". A Bias Square® ruler is helpful for cutting bias squares.

Thread: Use a good-quality, all-purpose cotton or cotton-covered polyester thread.

Needles: For machine piecing, a size 10/70 or 12/80 works well for most cottons.

For hand appliqué, choose a needle that will glide easily through the edges of the appliqué pieces. Size 10 (fine) to size 12 (very fine) needles work well.

Pins: Long, fine "quilters' pins" with glass or plastic heads are easy to handle. Small 1/2"- to 3/4"-long sequin pins work well for appliqué.

Scissors: Use your best scissors to cut fabric only. Use an older pair of scissors to cut paper, cardboard, and template plastic. Small, 4" scissors with sharp points are handy for clipping thread.

Sandpaper Board: This is an invaluable tool for accurately marking fabric. You can easily make one by adhering very fine sandpaper to a hard surface, such as wood, cardboard, poster board, or needlework mounting board. The sandpaper grabs the fabric and keeps it from slipping as you mark.

Template Plastic: Use clear or frosted plastic (available at quilt shops) to make durable, accurate templates.

Seam Ripper: Use this tool to remove stitches from incorrectly sewn seams.

Marking Tools: A variety of tools are available to mark fabrics when tracing around templates or marking quilting lines. Use a sharp #2 pencil or fine-lead mechanical pencil on lighter-colored fabrics, and a silver or yellow marking pencil on darker fabrics. Chalk pencils or chalk-wheel markers also make clear marks on fabric. Be sure to test your marking tool to make sure you can remove the marks easily.

ROTARY CUTTING

Instructions for quick-and-easy rotary cutting are provided wherever possible. All measurements include standard ¼"-wide seam allowances. For those unfamiliar with rotary cutting, a brief introduction is provided below. For more detailed information, see Donna Thomas's *Shortcuts: A Concise Guide to Rotary Cutting* (That Patchwork Place).

1. Fold the fabric and match selvages, aligning the crosswise and lengthwise grains as much as possible. Place the folded edge closest to you on the cutting mat. Align a square ruler along the folded edge of the fabric. Then place a long, straight ruler to the left of the square ruler, just covering the uneven raw edges of the left side of the fabric.

   Remove the square ruler and cut along the right edge of the long ruler, rolling the rotary cutter away from you. Discard this strip. (Reverse this procedure if you are left-handed.)

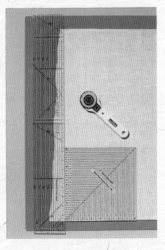

2. To cut strips, align the required measurement on the ruler with the newly cut edge of the fabric. For example, to cut a 3"-wide strip, place the 3" ruler mark on the edge of the fabric.

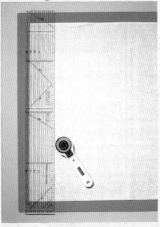

3. To cut squares, cut strips in the required widths. Trim away the selvage ends of the strip. Align the required measurement on the ruler with the left edge of the strip and cut a square. Continue cutting squares until you have the number needed.

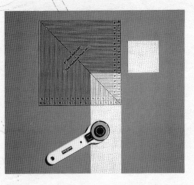

Half-Square Triangles

Make half-square triangles by cutting a square in half on the diagonal. The triangle's short sides are on the straight grain of fabric.

1. Cut squares, using the finished measurement of the triangle's short side, plus ⅞" for seam allowances.
2. Stack squares and cut once diagonally, corner to corner. Each square yields 2 triangles.

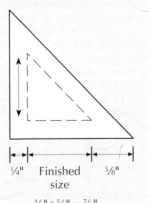
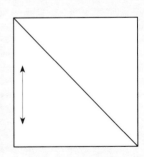

¼"   Finished   ⅝"
         size

¼" + ⅝" = ⅞"

Quarter-Square Triangles

Make quarter-square triangles by cutting a square in quarters on the diagonal. The long side of the triangle is on the straight grain of fabric.

1. Cut squares, using the finished measurement of the triangle's long side, plus 1¼" for seam allowances.
2. Stack squares and cut twice diagonally, from corner to corner. Each square yields 4 triangles.

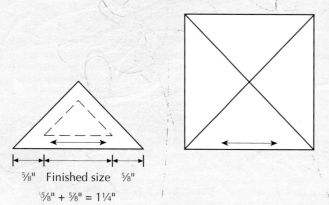

⅝" Finished size ⅝"
⅝" + ⅝" = 1¼"

MACHINE PIECING
Making Templates

Most blocks are designed for easy rotary cutting and quick piecing. Some blocks, however, require the use of templates for particular shapes. Templates for machine piecing include the required ¼"-wide seam allowances. Cut out the template on the outside line so that it includes the seam allowances. Be sure to mark the pattern name and grain-line arrow on the template.

Seam Allowances

The most important thing to remember about machine piecing is to maintain a consistent ¼"-wide seam allowance. Otherwise, the quilt block will not be the desired finished size. If that happens, the size of everything else in the quilt is affected, including alternate blocks, sashings, and borders. Measurements for all components of each quilt are based on blocks that finish accurately to the desired size plus ¼" on each edge for seam allowances.

Take the time to establish an exact ¼"-wide seam guide on your machine. Some machines have a special quilting foot that measures exactly ¼" from the center needle position to the edge of the foot. This feature allows you to use the edge of the presser foot to guide the fabric for a perfect ¼"-wide seam allowance.

If your machine doesn't have such a foot, create a seam guide by placing the edge of a piece of tape, moleskin, or a magnetic seam guide ¼" away from the needle.

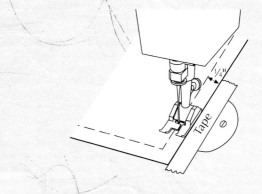

Chain Piecing

Chain piecing is an efficient system that saves time and thread.

1. Sew the first pair of pieces from cut edge to cut edge, using 12 to 15 stitches per inch. At the end of the seam, stop sewing but *do not* cut the thread.
2. Feed the next pair of pieces under the presser foot, as close as possible to the first pair. Continue feeding pieces through the machine without cutting the threads in between. There is no need to backstitch, since each seam will be crossed by another seam.
3. When all pieces have been sewn, remove the chain from the machine and clip the threads between the pieces.

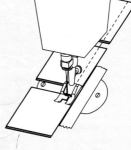

Chain piecing

Easing

If two pieces being sewn together are slightly different in size (less than ⅛"), pin the places where the two pieces should match, and in the middle if necessary, to distribute the excess fabric evenly. Sew the seam with the longer piece on the bottom. The feed dogs will ease the two pieces together.

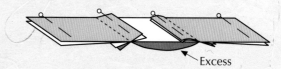

Excess

Pressing

The traditional rule in quiltmaking is to press seams to one side, toward the darker color wherever possible. Press the seam flat from the wrong side first, then press the seam in the desired direction from the right side. Press carefully to avoid distorting the shapes.

When joining two seamed units, plan ahead and press the seam allowances in opposite directions as shown. This reduces bulk and makes it easier to match seam lines. Where two seams meet, the seam allowances will butt against each other, making it easier to join units with perfectly matched seam intersections.

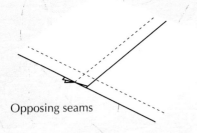

Opposing seams

Making Bias Squares

Many quilt patterns contain squares made from two contrasting half-square triangles. These are called bias squares or half-square triangle units. There are several different methods for making these units.

Using the bias strip–piecing method is especially useful for making large numbers of bias squares. This method is very accurate because seams are pressed after strips are pieced and before squares are cut. Instructions follow for making bias squares using Mary Hickey's method, as first shown in her book *Angle Antics* (That Patchwork Place).

An alternate method, cut-and-pieced squares, can be used when you need only a small number of units, or you need units in several different combinations. This method, which is explained on page 8, requires careful pressing after squares are stitched and cut.

Bias Strip–Piecing Method

You will need a Bias Square ruler to cut the units.
1. Layer the two fabrics with right sides facing up.
2. Establish a true bias line on the top fabric, using a ruler with a 45°-angle line. Cut bias strips parallel to the drawn line. Each quilt plan will specify how wide to cut the bias strips.

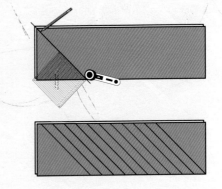

3. Sew the full-length bias strips together along the bias edges, offsetting the tops of the strips ¼" as shown. Alternating the fabrics, sew the strips into units of six to eight strips. Press seams toward the darker strips. When making 1½" or smaller bias squares, press seams open to distribute the bulk.

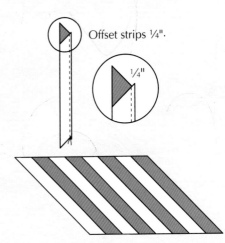

Offset strips ¼".

¼"

4. Position the Bias Square with the diagonal line on a seam line. Place a long ruler across the top to cut an even edge. The trimmed edge should be at a perfect 45° angle to the seam lines.

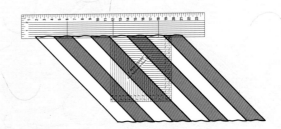

5. Cut a segment parallel to the first cut. Each quilt plan will specify how wide to cut this segment. Continue cutting segments into the specified widths, making sure to check and correct the angle at the edge after each cut.

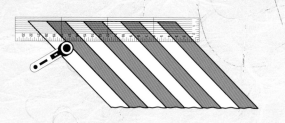

6. Sew the segments together, end to end, to create a long strip-pieced unit. This method prevents wasting triangles at the end of each unit. Be careful not to stretch the bias edges as you sew.
7. Place the Bias Square with the diagonal line on the seam line and one edge of the square on the bottom edge of the strip. Cut one side.

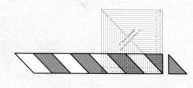

8. Place the diagonal line of the Bias Square on the seam line and the bottom edge of the ruler on the cut edge of the strip and cut the next bias square. The edges of the square should be lined up with the markings on the ruler to cut the required-size squares.

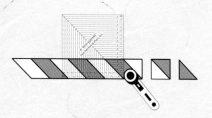

9. Continue cutting squares across the remainder of the strip until you have the number of bias squares required for the quilt you are making. Remember to align the diagonal line on the ruler with the seam line before each cut.

Cut-and-Pieced Squares

Remember to press carefully to avoid distorting the half-square triangle units.
1. Cut squares the size instructed in the quilt plan.
2. Draw a diagonal line from corner to corner on the back of the lightest fabric.

3. Place the square with the drawn line on top of another square, with right sides together. Sew ¼" away from the drawn line on both sides.

4. Cut on the drawn line. Press the seams toward the darker fabric and trim the "dog-ear" corners. Each pair of squares you sew together yields two half-square triangle units.

Trim

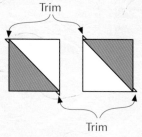

Trim

BASIC APPLIQUÉ

Instructions are provided for three different appliqué methods. Choose one of the following or use your own favorite method.

Making Templates

Templates made from clear plastic are more durable and accurate than those made from cardboard. Since you can see through the plastic, it is easy to trace the templates accurately.

Place template plastic over each pattern piece and trace with a fine-line permanent marker. Do not add seam allowances. Cut out the templates on the drawn lines. You need only one template for each different design. Mark the pattern name and grain-line arrow (if applicable) on the template.

Marking and Cutting Fabric

Place the template right side up on the right side of the appliqué fabric. Leave at least ½" between tracings if several pieces are needed. Cut out each fabric piece, adding a scant ¼"-wide seam allowance around each tracing. This seam allowance will be turned under to create the finished edge of the appliqué. On very small pieces, you may wish to add only ⅛" for easier handling.

The background fabric is usually a rectangle or square. Cut fabric the size and shape required for each project. It is better to cut the background an inch larger than needed in each direction to start, then trim it to the correct size after the appliqué has been sewn in place.

Place the background square or rectangle right side up over the pattern so that the design is centered. Lightly trace the design with a pencil. If your background fabric is dark, use a light box, or try taping the pattern to a window or storm door on a sunny day.

Traditional Appliqué Method

Before sewing appliqué pieces to the background, turn under the seam allowance, rolling the traced line to the back. Baste around each piece. Try looking at the right side of the piece while you turn the edge under, basting right along the fold. This helps to keep the piece neat and accurate as you concentrate on the smooth shape of the piece. If you keep your stitches near the fold, you will be sure to catch the seam allowance.

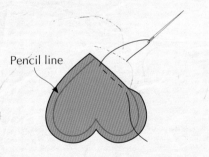

Pencil line

Do not turn under edges that will be covered by other appliqué pieces. They should lie flat under the covering appliqué piece.

Raw edge

Pin or baste the appliqué pieces to the background fabric. If you have trouble with threads tangling around pins as you sew, try placing the pins on the underside of your work.

Traditional Appliqué Stitch

The traditional appliqué stitch or blind stitch is appropriate for sewing all appliqué shapes, including sharp points and curves.

1. Tie a knot in a single strand of thread that is approximately 18" long.
2. Hide the knot by slipping the needle into the seam allowance from the wrong side of the appliqué piece, bringing it out on the fold line.
3. Work from right to left if you are right-handed, or left to right if you are left-handed.
4. Start the first stitch by moving the needle straight off the appliqué, inserting the needle into the background fabric. Let the needle travel under the background fabric, parallel to the edge of the appliqué, bringing it up about ⅛" away, along the pattern line.
5. As you bring the needle up, pierce the edge of the appliqué piece, catching only one or two threads of the folded edge.
6. Move the needle straight off the appliqué into the background fabric. Let your needle travel under the background, bringing it up about ⅛" away, again catching the edge of the appliqué.
7. Give the thread a slight tug and continue stitching.

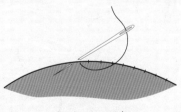

Appliqué stitch

8. To end your stitching, pull the needle through to the wrong side. Behind the appliqué piece, take two small stitches, making knots by taking your needle through the loops. Check the right side to see if the thread "shadows" through your background. If it does, take one more small stitch on the back side to direct the tail of the thread under the appliqué fabric.

Stitching Outside Points

As you stitch toward an outside point, start taking smaller stitches within 1/2" of the point. Trim the seam allowance or push the excess fabric under the point with the tip of your needle. Smaller stitches near the point will keep any frayed edges from escaping.

Place the last stitch on the first side very close to the point. Place the next stitch on the second side of the point. A stitch on each side, close to the point, will accent the outside point.

Stitching Along a Curve

Push the fabric under with the tip of your needle, smoothing it out along the folded edge before sewing.

Stitching Inside Points

Make your stitches smaller as you sew within 1/2" of the point. Stitch past the point, then return to the point to add one extra stitch to emphasize it. Come up through the appliqué, catching a little more fabric in the inside point (four or five threads instead of one or two). Make a straight stitch outward, going under the point to pull it in a little and emphasize its shape.

If your inside point frays, use a few close stitches to tack the fabric down securely. If your thread matches your appliqué fabric, these stitches will blend in with the edge of the shape.

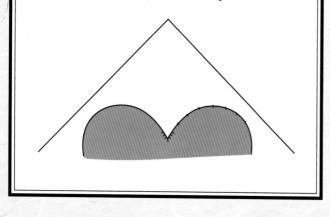

Alternate Appliqué Methods

Needle-Turn Appliqué

This method moves directly from cutting to the appliqué stitch. You do not turn under and baste the seam allowances.

1. Using a plastic template, trace the design onto the right side of the appliqué fabric.
2. Cut out the fabric piece, adding a scant 1/4"-wide seam allowance all around.
3. Position the appliqué piece on the background fabric; pin or baste in place.
4. Starting on a straight edge, use the tip of the needle to gently turn under the seam allowance, about 1/2" at a time. Hold the turned seam allowance firmly between the thumb and first finger of your left hand (reverse if left-handed) as you stitch the appliqué to the background. Use a longer needle—a Sharp or milliner's needle—to help you control the seam allowance and turn it under neatly.

Note: Stitches in illustration show placement. They should *not* show in completed work.

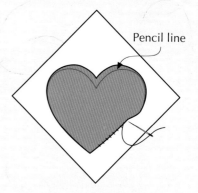

Pencil line

Freezer-Paper Method

Use freezer paper (plastic coated on one side) to help make perfectly shaped appliqués. You can trace around a template or simply trace the design onto the freezer paper. The seam allowances are then turned over the freezer-paper edges and basted or glued to the back side before appliquéing the shape to the background.

1. Place freezer paper, plastic side down, on top of the pattern and trace the design with a sharp pencil.

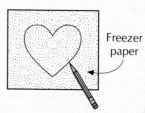

Freezer paper

2. Cut out the freezer paper design on the pencil line. Do not add seam allowances.

3. With the plastic-coated side against the wrong side of the fabric, iron the freezer paper in place, using a hot, dry iron.

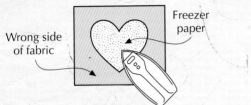

Wrong side of fabric

Freezer paper

4. Cut out the shape, adding ¼"-wide seam allowances all around the outside edge of the freezer paper.

5. Turn and baste the seam allowance over the freezer-paper edges by hand, or use a glue stick. (Clip inside points and fold outside points.)

Clip corner.

GLUE

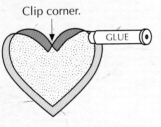

6. Pin or baste the design to the background fabric. Appliqué the design.

7. Remove any basting stitches. Cut a small slit in the background fabric behind the appliqué and remove the freezer paper with tweezers. If you used a glue stick, soak the piece in warm water for a few minutes before removing the freezer paper.

Invisible Machine Appliqué

If you prefer machine appliqué, try Roxi Eppler's Smoothstitch® techniques, featured in her book *Smoothstitch Quilts: Easy Machine Appliqué* (That Patchwork Place). Her invisible machine-appliqué techniques can be applied to any of the appliqué projects in this book.

Making Bias Stems

Bias stems are easy to make with the help of metal or nylon bias press bars.

1. Cut fabric into ¾"-wide bias strips, using a rotary cutter and clear acrylic ruler.

2. Fold the strip in half lengthwise and stitch ¼" from the folded edge. This will leave a ⅛"-wide seam allowance.

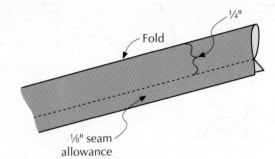

Fold

¼"

⅛" seam allowance

3. Insert a ¼" bias bar, roll the seam to the underside, and press. Remove the bias bar.

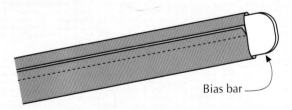

Bias bar

ASSEMBLING THE QUILT TOP

Squaring up Blocks

When your blocks are complete, take the time to square them up. Use a large square ruler to measure your blocks and make sure they are the desired size plus an extra 1/4" on each edge for seam allowances. For example, if you are making 6" blocks, they should all measure 6½" before you sew them together. Trim the larger blocks to match the size of the smallest one. Be sure to trim all four sides; otherwise your block will be lopsided.

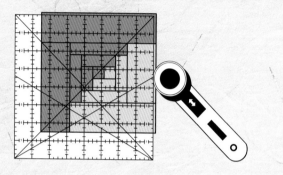

If your blocks are not the required finished size, you will have to adjust all the other components of the quilt accordingly.

Making Straight-Set Quilts

1. Arrange the blocks as shown in the quilt plan provided with each quilt.
2. Sew blocks together in horizontal rows; press the seams in opposite directions from row to row.

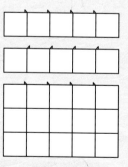

Straight-Set Quilts

3. Sew the rows together, making sure to match the seams between the blocks.

Making Diagonally Set Quilts

1. Arrange the blocks, side triangles, and corner triangles as shown in the quilt plan provided with each quilt.
2. Sew the blocks together in diagonal rows; press the seams in opposite directions from row to row.
3. Sew the rows together, making sure to match the seams between the blocks. Sew the corner triangles on last.

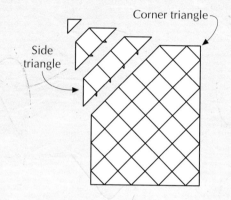

Diagonally Set Quilts

Adding Borders

For best results, do not cut border strips and sew them directly to the quilt sides without measuring first. The edges of a quilt often measure slightly longer than the distance through the quilt center, due to stretching during construction. Instead, measure the quilt top through the center in both directions to determine how long to cut the border strips. This step ensures that the finished quilt will be as straight and as "square" as possible, without wavy edges.

Plain border strips are commonly cut along the crosswise grain and seamed where extra length is needed. Borders cut from the lengthwise grain of fabric require extra yardage, but seaming the required length is then unnecessary.

You may add borders that have straight-cut corners, corner squares, or mitered corners.

Straight-Cut Borders

1. Measure the length of the quilt top through the center. Cut border strips to that measurement, piecing as necessary; mark the center of the quilt edges and the border strips. Pin the borders to the sides of the quilt top, matching the center marks and ends and easing as necessary. Sew the border strips in place. Press seams toward the border.

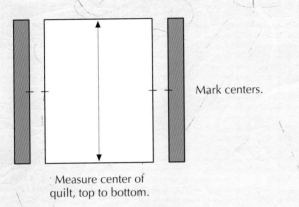

Mark centers.

Measure center of quilt, top to bottom.

2. Measure the width of the quilt top through the center, including the side borders just added. Cut border strips to that measurement, piecing as necessary; mark the center of the quilt edges and the border strips. Pin the borders to the top and bottom edges of the quilt top, matching the center marks and ends and easing as necessary; stitch. Press seams toward the border.

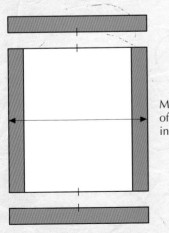

Measure center of quilt, side to side, including borders.

Mark centers.

Borders with Corner Squares

1. Measure the width and length of the quilt top through the center. Cut border strips to those measurements, piecing as necessary. Mark the center of the quilt edges and the border strips. Pin the side borders to opposite sides of the quilt top, matching centers and ends and easing as necessary. Sew the side border strips; press seams toward the border.

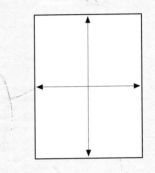

2. Cut corner squares of the required size (the cut width of the border strips). Sew one corner square to each end of the remaining two border strips; press seams toward the border strips. Pin the border strips to the top and bottom edges of the quilt top. Match centers, seams between the border strip and corner square, and ends, easing as necessary; stitch. Press seams toward the border.

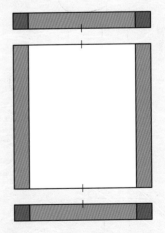

Borders with Mitered Corners

1. First estimate the finished outside dimensions of your quilt, including borders. Border strips should be cut to this length plus at least ½" for seam allowances; it's safer to add 3" to 4" to give yourself some leeway. For example, if your quilt top measures 35½" x 50½" across the center and you want a 5"-wide finished border, your quilt will measure 45" x 60" after the borders are attached.

Note: If your quilt has multiple borders, sew the individual strips together and treat the resulting unit as a single border strip.

2. Fold the quilt in half and mark the center of the quilt edges. Fold each border strip in half and mark the center with a pin.

3. Measure the length and width of the quilt top across the center. Note the measurements.

4. Place a pin at each end of the side border strips to mark the length of the quilt top. Repeat with the top and bottom borders.

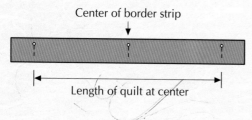

Center of border strip

Length of quilt at center

5. Pin the borders to the quilt top, matching the centers. Line up the pins at each end of the border strip with the edges of the quilt. Stitch, beginning and ending the stitching ¼" from the raw edges of the quilt top. Repeat with the remaining borders.

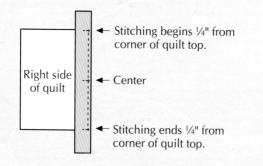

Stitching begins ¼" from corner of quilt top.

Right side of quilt

Center

Stitching ends ¼" from corner of quilt top.

6. Lay the first corner to be mitered on the ironing board. Fold under one border strip at a 45° angle to the other strip. Press and pin.

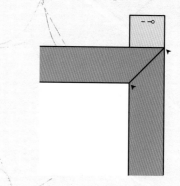

7. Fold the quilt with right sides together, lining up the edges of the border. If necessary, use a ruler to draw a pencil line on the crease to make the line more visible. Stitch on the crease, sewing from the corner to the outside edge.

Pressed crease

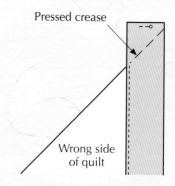

Wrong side of quilt

8. Press the seam open and trim away excess border strips, leaving a ¼"-wide seam allowance.

9. Repeat with remaining corners.

PREPARING TO QUILT

Marking the Quilting Lines

Whether or not to mark the quilting designs depends upon the type of quilting you will be doing. Marking is not necessary if you plan to quilt in-the-ditch or outline quilt a uniform distance from seam lines. For more complex quilting designs, mark the quilt top before the quilt is layered with batting and backing.

Choose a marking tool that will be visible on your fabric and test it on fabric scraps to be sure the marks can be removed easily. See "Marking Tools" on page 4 for options. Masking tape can also be used to mark straight quilting. Tape only small sections at a time and remove the tape when you stop at the end of the day; otherwise, the sticky residue may be difficult to remove from the fabric.

Layering the Quilt

The quilt "sandwich" consists of backing, batting, and the quilt top.

Cut the quilt backing at least 4" larger than the quilt top all the way around. For large quilts, it is usually necessary to sew two or three lengths of fabric together to make a backing of the required size. Trim away the selvages before piecing the lengths together. Press the backing seams open to make quilting easier.

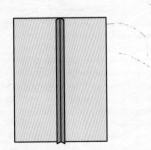

Two lengths of fabric seamed in the center

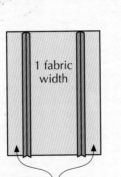

1 fabric width

Partial fabric width

Batting comes packaged in standard bed sizes, or it can be purchased by the yard. Several weights or thicknesses are available. Thick battings are fine for tied quilts and comforters; a thinner batting is better, however, if you intend to quilt by hand or machine.

To put it all together:

1. Spread the backing, wrong side up, on a flat, clean surface. Anchor it with pins or masking tape. Be careful not to stretch the backing out of shape.
2. Spread the batting over the backing, smoothing out any wrinkles.
3. Place the pressed quilt top on top of the batting. Smooth out any wrinkles and make sure the edges of the quilt top are parallel to the edges of the backing.
4. Starting in the center, baste with needle and thread and work diagonally to each corner. Continue basting in a grid of horizontal and vertical lines 6"–8" apart. Finish by basting around the edges.

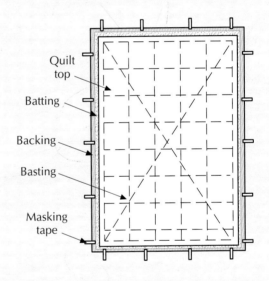

Quilt top

Batting

Backing

Basting

Masking tape

Note: For machine quilting, you may baste the layers with #2 rust-proof safety pins. Place pins about 6" to 8" apart, away from the area you intend to quilt.

QUILTING TECHNIQUES

Hand Quilting

To quilt by hand, you will need short, sturdy needles (called "Betweens"), quilting thread, and a thimble to fit the middle finger of your sewing hand. Most quilters also use a frame or hoop to support their work. Use the smallest needle you can comfortably handle; the finer the needle, the smaller your stitches will be.

1. Thread your needle with a single strand of quilting thread about 18" long; make a small knot and insert the needle in the top layer about 1" from the place where you want to start stitching. Pull the needle out at the point where quilting will begin and gently pull the thread until the knot pops through the fabric and into the batting.

2. Take small, evenly spaced stitches through all three quilt layers.

3. Rock the needle up and down through all layers, until you have three or four stitches on the needle. Place your other hand underneath the quilt so you can feel the needle point with the tip of your finger when a stitch is taken.

4. To end a line of quilting, make a small knot close to the last stitch; then, backstitch, running the thread a needle's length through the batting. Gently pull the thread until the knot pops into the batting; clip the thread at the quilt's surface.

For more information on hand quilting, refer to *Loving Stitches* by Jeana Kimball (That Patchwork Place).

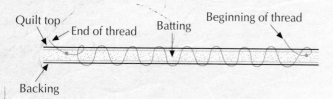

Quilt top — End of thread — Batting — Beginning of thread
Backing

Machine Quilting

Machine quilting is suitable for all types of quilts, from crib to full-size bed quilts. With machine quilting, you can quickly complete quilts that might otherwise languish on the shelves.

Marking is only necessary if you need to follow a grid or a complex pattern. It is not necessary if you plan to quilt in-the-ditch, outline quilt a uniform distance from seam lines, or free-motion quilt in a random pattern.

1. For straight-line quilting, it is extremely helpful to have a walking foot to help feed the quilt layers through the machine without shifting or puckering. Some machines have a built-in walking foot; other machines require a separate attachment.

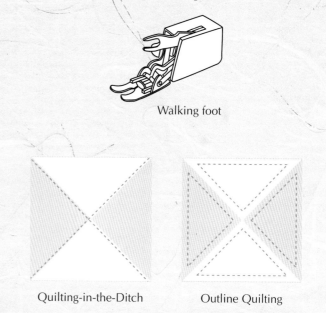

Walking foot

Quilting-in-the-Ditch   Outline Quilting

2. For free-motion quilting, you need a darning foot and the ability to drop the feed dogs on the machine. With free-motion quilting, you do not turn the fabric under the needle but instead guide the fabric in the direction of the design. Use free-motion quilting to outline quilt a pattern in the fabric or to create stippling and many other curved designs.

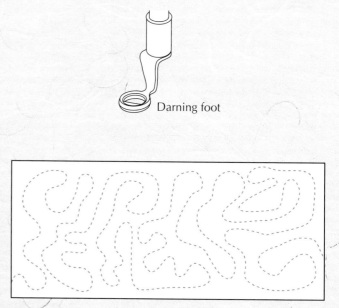

Darning foot

Free-Motion Quilting

FINISHING

Binding

Bindings can be made from straight-grain or bias-grain strips of fabric. For a French double-fold binding, cut strips 2½" wide.

Note: If you want to attach a sleeve or rod pocket to the back of the quilt, see page 18 for instructions to make the sleeve before you attach the binding.

To cut straight-grain binding strips:

Cut 2½"-wide strips across the width of the fabric. You will need enough strips to go around the perimeter of the quilt plus 10" for seams and the corners in a mitered fold.

To cut bias-grain binding strips:

1. Fold a square of fabric on the diagonal.

Bias fold

OR

Fold a ½-yard piece as shown in the diagrams below, paying careful attention to the location of the lettered corners.

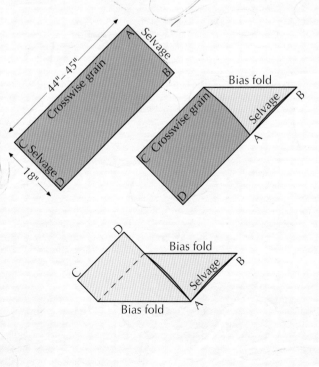

2. Cut strips 2½" wide, cutting perpendicular to the folds as shown.

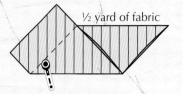
½ yard of fabric

Bias fold

Square of fabric

To attach binding:

1. Sew strips, right sides together, to make one long piece of binding. Press seams open.

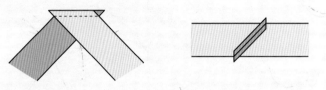

   If you cut strips on the straight grain, join strips at right angles and stitch across the corner as shown. Trim excess fabric and press seams open.

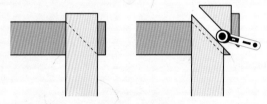

Joining Straight-Cut Strips

2. Fold the strip in half lengthwise, wrong sides together, and press.
3. Turn under ¼" at a 45° angle at one end of the strip and press. Turning the end under at an angle distributes the bulk so you won't have a lump where the two ends of the binding meet.

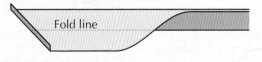
Fold line

4. Trim batting and backing even with the quilt top.
5. Starting on one side of the quilt and using a ⅜"-wide seam allowance, stitch the binding to the quilt, keeping the raw edges even with the quilt-top edge. End the stitching ⅜" from the corner of the quilt and backstitch. Clip the thread.

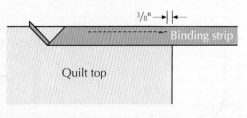
⅜"
Binding strip
Quilt top

6. Turn the quilt so that you will be stitching down the next side. Fold the binding up, away from the quilt.

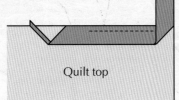

Quilt top

7. Fold the binding back down onto itself, parallel with the edge of the quilt top. Begin stitching ³/₈" from the edge, backstitching to secure.

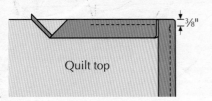

Quilt top

↕ ³/₈"

8. Repeat on the remaining edges and corners of the quilt. When you reach the beginning of the binding, overlap the beginning stitches by about 1" and cut away any excess binding, trimming the end at a 45° angle. Tuck the end of the binding into the fold and finish the seam.

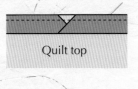

Quilt top

9. Fold the binding over the raw edges of the quilt to the back, with the folded edge covering the row of machine stitching, and blindstitch in place. A miter will form at each corner. Blindstitch the mitered corners in place.

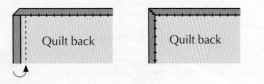

Quilt back   Quilt back

Adding a Sleeve

If you plan to display your finished quilt on the wall, be sure to add a hanging sleeve to hold the rod.

1. Using leftover fabric from the front or a piece of muslin, cut a strip 6" to 8" wide and 1" shorter than the width of the quilt at the top edge. Fold the ends under ½", then ½" again, and stitch.

2. Fold the fabric strip in half lengthwise, wrong sides together, and baste the raw edges to the top edge of the back of your quilt. The top edge of the sleeve will be secured when the binding is sewn onto the quilt.

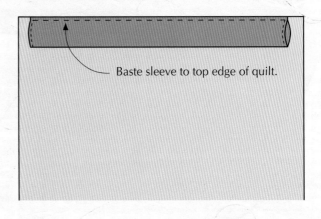

Baste sleeve to top edge of quilt.

3. Finish the sleeve after the binding has been attached by blindstitching the bottom of the sleeve in place. Push the bottom edge of the sleeve up just a bit to provide a little give so the hanging rod does not put strain on the quilt itself.

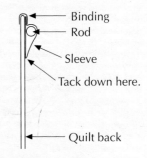

— Binding
— Rod

— Sleeve

— Tack down here.

— Quilt back

Signing Your Quilt

Be sure to sign and date your quilt. Future generations will be interested to know more than just who made it and when. Labels can be as elaborate or as simple as you desire. The information can be handwritten, typed, or embroidered. Be sure to include the name of the quilt, your name, your city and state, the date, the name of the recipient if it is a gift, and any other interesting or important information about the quilt.

Princess Feather with Birds

By Donna Hanson Eines

Princess Feather with Birds by Donna Hanson Eines, 1994, Edmonds, Washington, 80$1/2$" x 80$1/2$".

DONNA HANSON EINES

DONNA HAS BEEN QUILTING SINCE 1974, AND HER QUILTS HAVE WON NUMEROUS RIBBONS AND AWARDS. THEY HAVE APPEARED IN SEVERAL MAGAZINES, INCLUDING *QUILTING TODAY*, *GOOD HOUSEKEEPING*, AND *LADY'S CIRCLE PATCHWORK QUILTS*, AND ON THE COVER OF *QUILTER'S NEWSLETTER MAGAZINE* AND TWO SHIRLEY THOMPSON QUILTING DESIGN BOOKS. HER "CURRANT AND COXCOMB" QUILT HAS WON SEVERAL AWARDS, INCLUDING BEST OF SHOW AT THE EVERGREEN STATE FAIR, AND IT APPEARED IN THE FIRST VOLUME OF *QUILTED FOR CHRISTMAS*, PUBLISHED IN 1994.

IN 1985, A ONE-WOMAN SHOW OF DONNA'S QUILTS WAS HELD AT THE ANNUAL COUPEVILLE, WASHINGTON, ARTS AND CRAFTS FESTIVAL. DONNA WAS SELECTED, ALONG WITH HER "BASKET MEDALLION" QUILT, TO REPRESENT PRESENT-DAY QUILTERS AND QUILTS IN THE BOOK *WOMEN AND THEIR QUILTS*, A *WASHINGTON STATE CENTENNIAL TRIBUTE*, BY NANCYANN JOHANSON TWELKER.

WHEN IT COMES TO QUILTING, DONNA IS VERY MUCH A TRADITIONALIST. SHE ENJOYS MAKING QUILTS WITH COMPONENTS REMINISCENT OF ANTIQUE QUILTS AND BASES HER COLOR SELECTIONS ON THOSE POPULAR IN DAYS PAST. "PRINCESS FEATHER WITH BIRDS," WHICH WON BEST OF SHOW AT THE 1994 EVERGREEN STATE FAIR, IS AN EXCELLENT EXAMPLE OF HER DESIGNING STYLE. YOU MIGHT SAY THAT DONNA LIVES TO QUILT—THAT IS, TO COVER THE SURFACE OF A COMPLETED DESIGN WITH EXQUISITE QUILTING. IT IS HER GREATEST JOY IN THE PROCESS. "PRINCESS FEATHER WITH BIRDS" IS NO EXCEPTION: TRAPUNTO DESIGNS BETWEEN EACH FEATHER AND DIAGONAL LINES SPACED $1/4$" APART ACROSS THE QUILT LEND INTRIGUING SURFACE TEXTURE. COLOR, DESIGN, AND FINE HAND QUILTING MAKE THIS QUILT A MASTERPIECE!

Quilt Plan

Quilt Size: 80½" x 80½"

Materials: 44"-wide fabric

3 yds. muslin for center block and middle border

2½ yds. red solid for feathers, large-medium-small-half flowers, flower buds, outer swags, and berries

1½ yds. green print for center flower, baskets, vines, inner swags, and leaves

1⅛ yds. gold solid for flower centers and birds

1⅜ yds. beige solid for inner border and half squares in middle border

4¾ yds. khaki solid for outer borders and binding

5 yds. for backing

84" x 84" piece of batting

6 to 24 skeins of six-strand, gold embroidery floss (Actual number of skeins required depends on the density of your French knots.)

Tissue paper or butcher paper

Template plastic

Cutting

Use the appliqué templates on pages 24–29 and the placement guides on the pullout pattern insert at the back of the book. Make templates and cut from the appropriate fabrics, following the "Basic Appliqué" directions that begin on page 8.

From the muslin, cut:
1 square, 35½" x 35½", for center square;
4 strips, each 9" x 60½", for middle border.

From the red solid, cut:
8 of Template 1 (feather);
1 of Template 2 (large flower);
4 of Template 6 (medium flower);
24 of Template 8 (small flower);
32 of Template 11 (outer swag);
4 of Template 13 (outer corner swag);
8 of Template 16 (flower bud);
4 of Template 18 (half flower);
72 of Template 20 (berry).

From the green print, cut:
1 of Template 3 (center ring of large flower);
48 of Template 5 (leaf);
48 of Template 5 reversed (leaf);
4 of Template 14 (flower pot handle);
4 of Template 14 reversed (flower pot handle);
4 of Template 15 (flower pot);
32 of Template 10 (inner swag);
4 of Template 12 (inner corner swag);
1"-wide bias strips to total 440" for vines.

From the gold solid, cut:
1 of Template 4 (center of large flower);
4 of Template 7 (center of medium flower);
24 of Template 9 (center of small flower);
8 of Template 17 (bird);
8 of Template 17 reversed (bird);
4 of Template 19 (center of half flower).

From the beige solid, cut:
4 strips, each 4½" x 43½", for inner border;
2 squares, each 12⅞" x 12⅞"; cut squares once
diagonally to yield 4 triangles for the centers
of the middle borders.

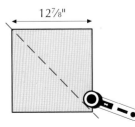

From the khaki solid, cut:
4 strips, each 10½" x 80½", for outer borders; set
the remaining fabric aside for the binding.

Assembling the Center Block

Use pieces 1–4.

1. Referring to the illustration below and using the appliqué templates for the feather and center flower, make a full-size paper pattern of the center square, including placement lines. Draw a 35½" square on the tissue paper. Fold the square in half, in half again, then on the diagonal as shown to crease.

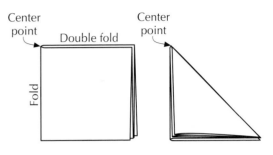

Position the feathers so that the ends are tucked under the center flower and the outer points are approximately ⅝" from the cut edges of the square.

Make a paper pattern.

2. Fold the muslin background square as shown for the paper pattern and finger-press the folds to crease.
3. Lay the background square on the paper pattern, lining up the folds with the placement lines, to center the design in the square. Trace the design onto the muslin, using a sharp, fine pencil.
4. Prepare the appliqué pieces, using one of the appliqué methods on pages 9–11 or your favorite method.
5. Position and appliqué the pieces in numerical order on the background square.

Assembling and Adding the Inner Border

Use pieces 5–9, bias strips for the vines, and the "Inner Border Placement Guide" on the pullout pattern insert at the back of the book.

1. Fold each beige inner border strip in half crosswise and finger-press the fold.
2. Remove the pattern sheet with the "Inner Border Placement Guide" from the back of the book and trace it onto tissue paper. Turn the paper pattern over, and if you cannot easily see the lines from the wrong side, place the tracing face down on a light table or against a window and trace the lines onto the wrong side of the paper. Turn the paper pattern to the right side.
3. Place an inner border strip on top of the pattern at the fold line. Trace the design onto the border strip, using a sharp pencil. Reverse the pattern and trace the second half in the remaining half of the border strip. Repeat with the remaining inner border strips.

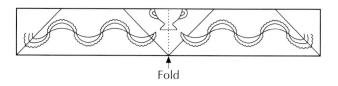

Fold

4. Prepare the appliqué pieces, using one of the appliqué methods on pages 9–11 or your favorite method.
5. To prepare the bias strips for the vines, fold the 1"-wide green bias strips in half with wrong sides together. Stitch 3/8" from the fold, leaving a 1/8"-wide seam allowance.

3/8"

6. Insert a 3/8"-wide bias bar and press as shown in "Making Bias Stems" on page 11.
7. Appliqué the leaves, the vines, and then the remaining pieces in numerical order.
8. Sew the completed borders to the center square, following the directions for "Borders with Mitered Corners" on page 14.

Assembling and Adding the Middle Border

Use pieces 10–15 and the "Middle Border Placement Guide" located on the pullout pattern insert at the back of the book.

1. Fold each muslin middle border strip in half crosswise and finger-press the fold.
2. Remove the pattern sheets with the "Middle Border Placement Guide" from the back of the book and trace it onto tissue paper, joining sections 1 and 2. Turn the paper pattern over, and if you cannot easily see the lines from the wrong side, place the tracing face down on a light table or against a window and trace the lines onto the wrong side of the paper. Turn the pattern to the right side.
3. Place a middle border strip on top of the pattern at the fold line. Trace the design onto the border strip, using a sharp pencil. Reverse the pattern and trace the second half in the remaining half of the border strip. Repeat with the remaining middle border strips.

Fold

4. Sew each inner swag piece to an outer swag piece, using a 1/4"-wide seam allowance.

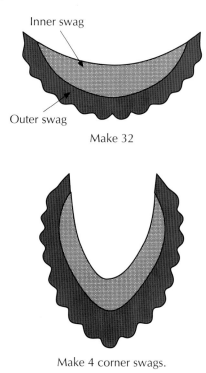

Inner swag

Outer swag

Make 32

Make 4 corner swags.

5. Position the swags on the borders and appliqué in place, leaving the corner swags to be appliquéd after the border is attached to the center square and inner border unit.

6. Trace the flower pot and handle onto each large beige triangle, following the placement lines on the "Middle Border Placement Guide." Appliqué a flower pot and 2 flower-pot handles to each triangle, then appliqué a completed triangle to each border strip, following the placement lines.

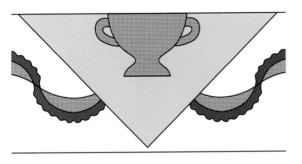

7. Turn the completed border strips over and trim away the border fabric behind the triangles, leaving a ¼" allowance of fabric.

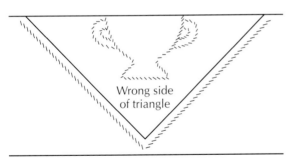

Wrong side of triangle

8. Sew the completed middle borders to the quilt top, mitering the corners as before.

9. Position and appliqué the corner swags.

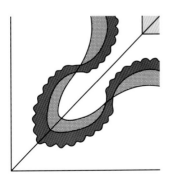

Appliqué corner swags.

Assembling and Adding the Outer Border

Use piece 5 and pieces 16–20 and the "Outer Border Placement Guide" located on the pullout pattern insert at the back of the book.

1. Fold each khaki outer border strip in half crosswise and finger-press the fold.

2. Remove the pattern sheet with the "Outer Border Placement Guide" from the back of the book and trace it onto tissue paper. Turn the paper pattern over, and if you cannot easily see the lines from the wrong side, place the tracing face down on a light table or against a window and trace the lines onto the wrong side of the paper. Turn the paper pattern to the right side.

3. Place an outer border strip on top of the pattern at the fold line. Trace the design onto the border strip, using a sharp pencil. Reverse the pattern and trace the second half in the remaining half of the border strip. Repeat with the remaining outer border strips.

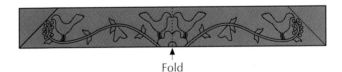

Fold

4. Appliqué the flower buds and leaves, then add the remaining pieces in numerical order. Before stitching down the berries completely, tuck a bit of fiberfill inside to add dimension.

5. Sew the completed borders to the quilt top, mitering the corners as before.

Finishing

1. Embellish all flower centers with French knots, using 6 strands of embroidery floss. You may use only a few knots, or you can cover the surface completely. It's your choice.

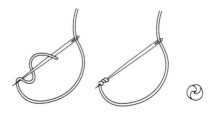

French Knot

2. Mark the feather quilting design (page 29) between the red feathers in the quilt center. Mark a diagonal grid in the background and mark quilting lines on appliqués as shown on the appliqué templates.
3. Layer the quilt top with batting and backing; baste.
4. Quilt on the marked lines.(See page 16.)
5. From the remaining khaki fabric, cut and prepare enough bias strips to total 9 yards as shown on page 17. Bind the edges of the quilt. (See page 17–18).
6. Sign your quilt. (See page 18.)

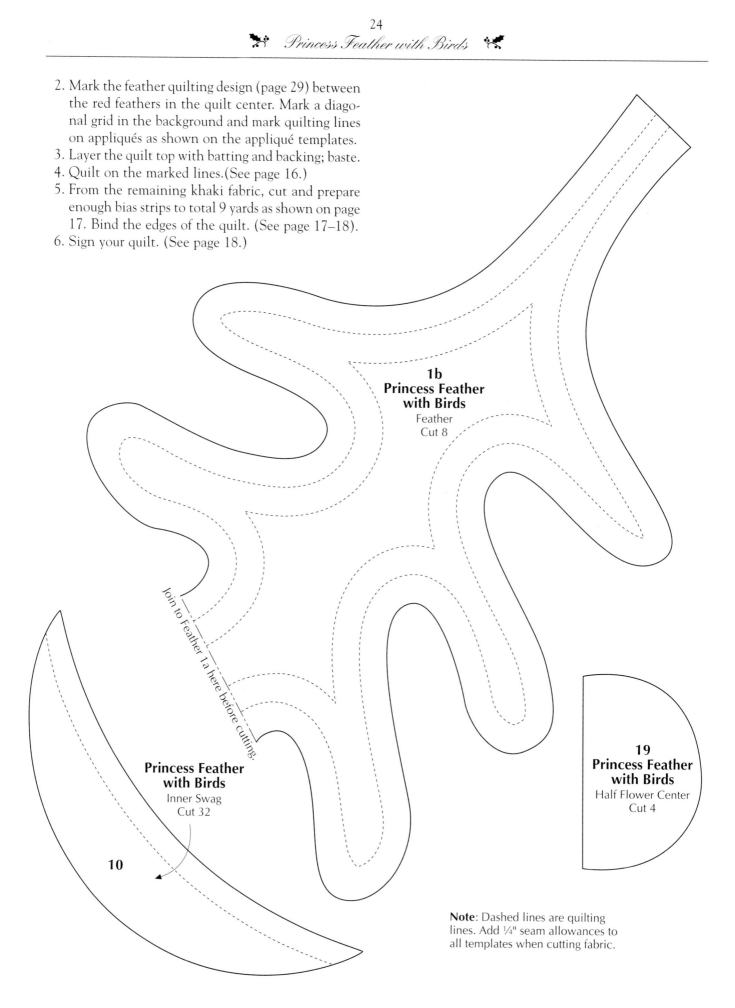

**1b
Princess Feather
with Birds**
Feather
Cut 8

Join to Feather 1a here before cutting.

**Princess Feather
with Birds**
Inner Swag
Cut 32

10

**19
Princess Feather
with Birds**
Half Flower Center
Cut 4

Note: Dashed lines are quilting lines. Add ¼" seam allowances to all templates when cutting fabric.

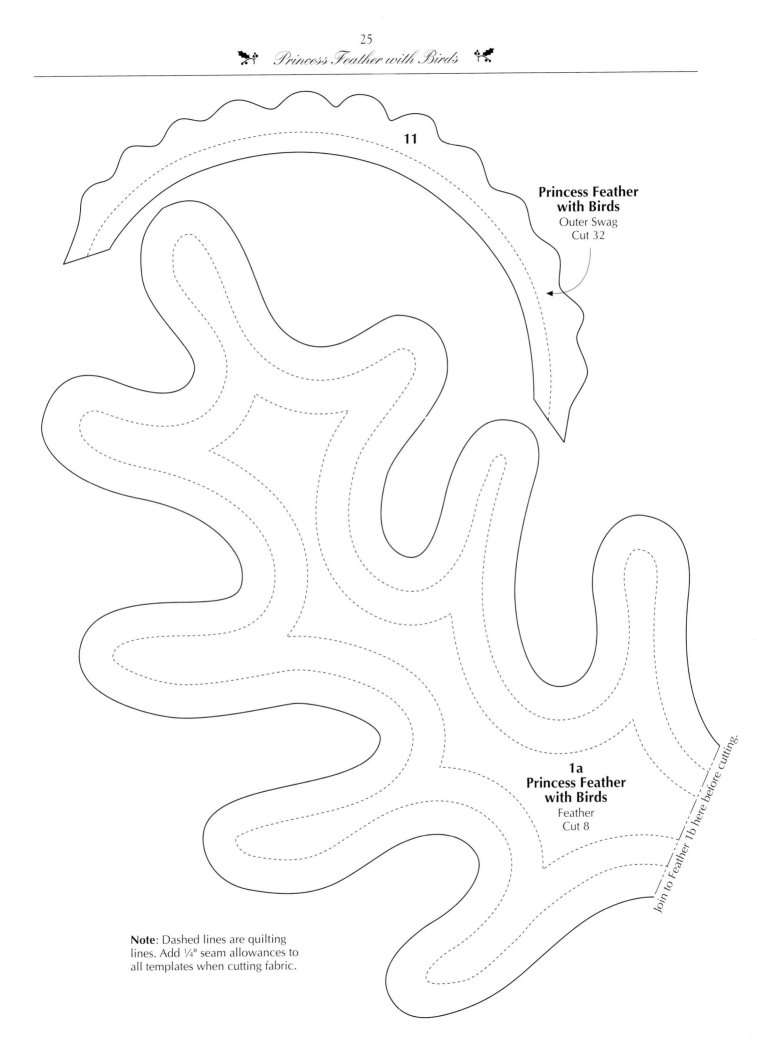

11

**Princess Feather
with Birds**
Outer Swag
Cut 32

**1a
Princess Feather
with Birds**
Feather
Cut 8

Join to Feather 1b here before cutting.

Note: Dashed lines are quilting
lines. Add ¼" seam allowances to
all templates when cutting fabric.

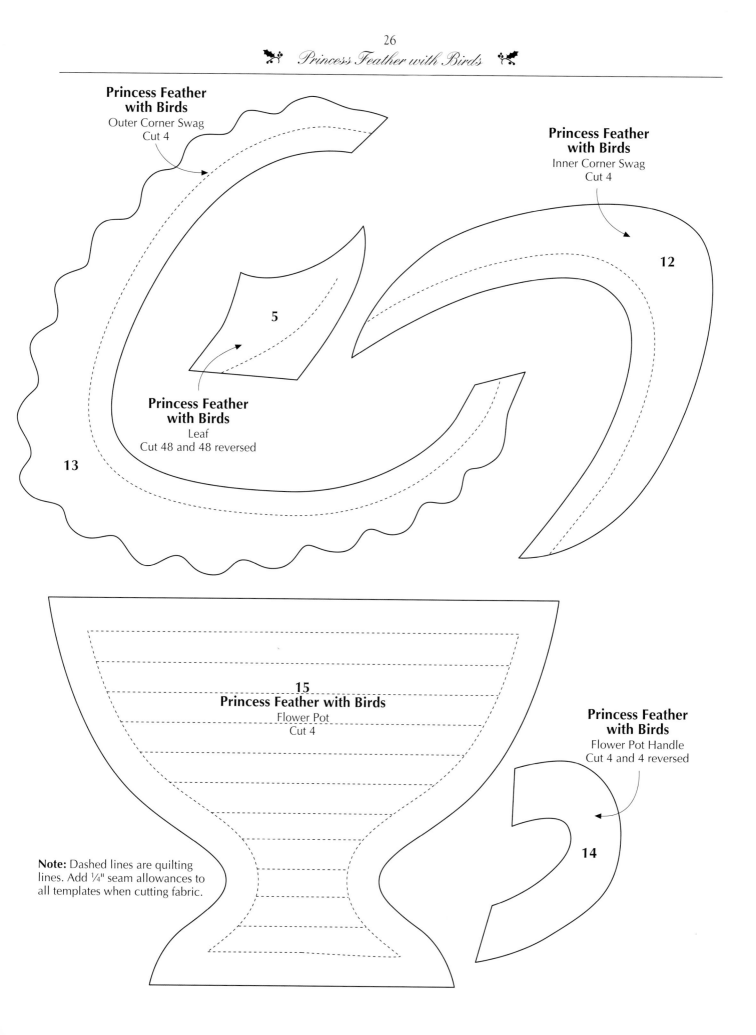

**Princess Feather
with Birds**
Outer Corner Swag
Cut 4

**Princess Feather
with Birds**
Inner Corner Swag
Cut 4

12

5

**Princess Feather
with Birds**
Leaf
Cut 48 and 48 reversed

13

**15
Princess Feather with Birds**
Flower Pot
Cut 4

**Princess Feather
with Birds**
Flower Pot Handle
Cut 4 and 4 reversed

14

Note: Dashed lines are quilting lines. Add ¼" seam allowances to all templates when cutting fabric.

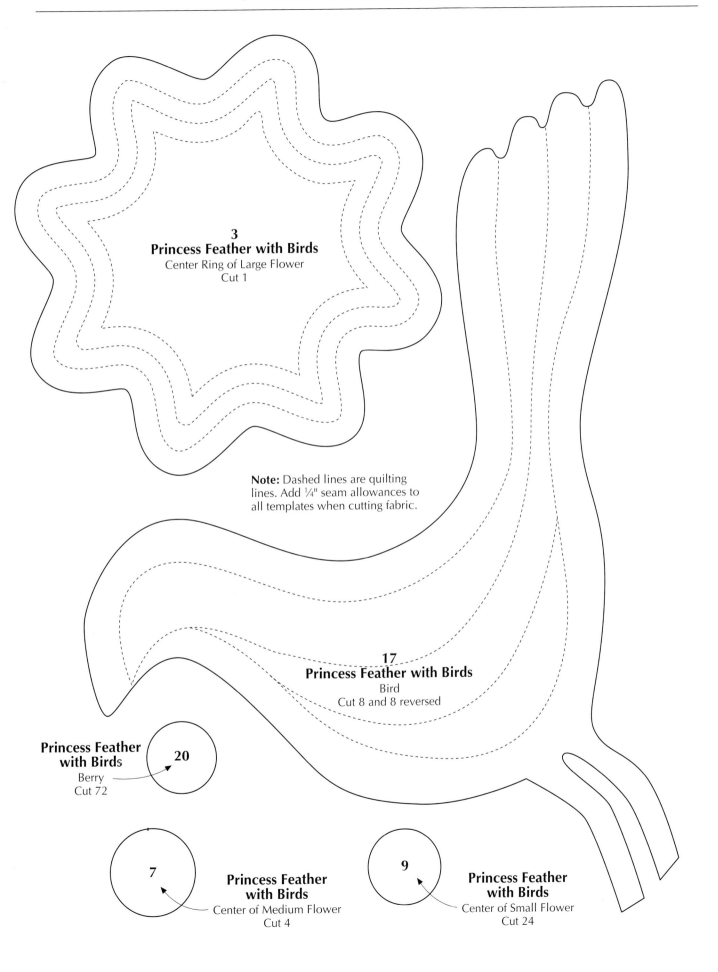

3
Princess Feather with Birds
Center Ring of Large Flower
Cut 1

Note: Dashed lines are quilting lines. Add ¼" seam allowances to all templates when cutting fabric.

17
Princess Feather with Birds
Bird
Cut 8 and 8 reversed

Princess Feather with Birds
Berry
Cut 72

20

7

Princess Feather with Birds
Center of Medium Flower
Cut 4

9

Princess Feather with Birds
Center of Small Flower
Cut 24

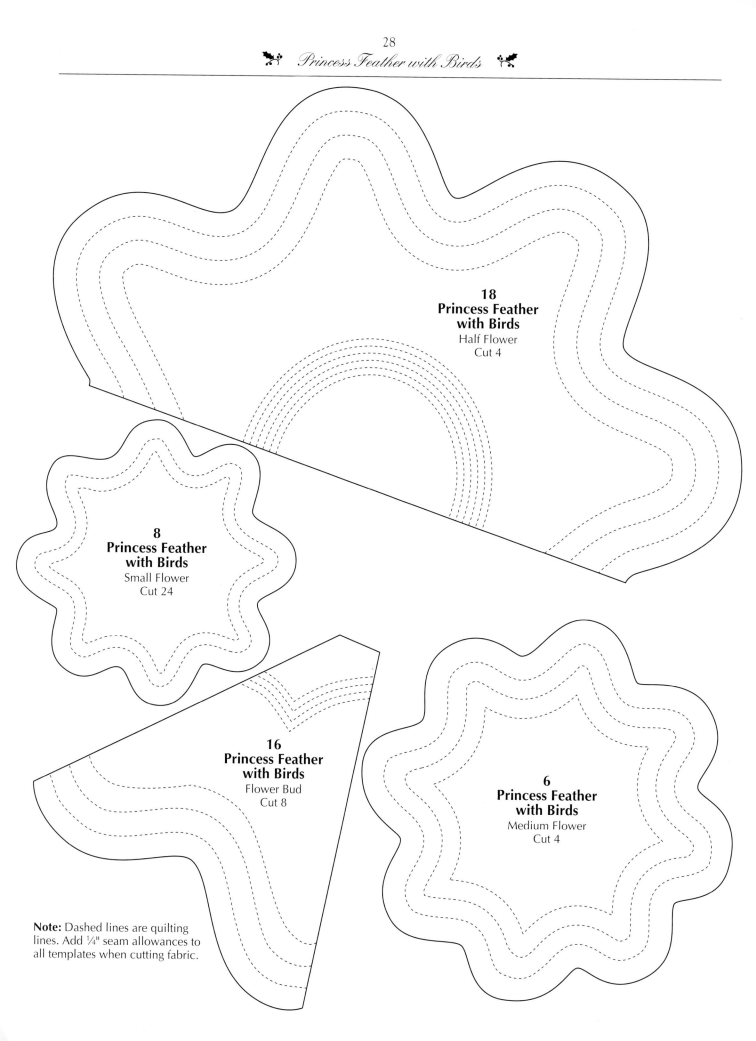

**18
Princess Feather
with Birds**
Half Flower
Cut 4

**8
Princess Feather
with Birds**
Small Flower
Cut 24

**16
Princess Feather
with Birds**
Flower Bud
Cut 8

**6
Princess Feather
with Birds**
Medium Flower
Cut 4

Note: Dashed lines are quilting
lines. Add ¼" seam allowances to
all templates when cutting fabric.

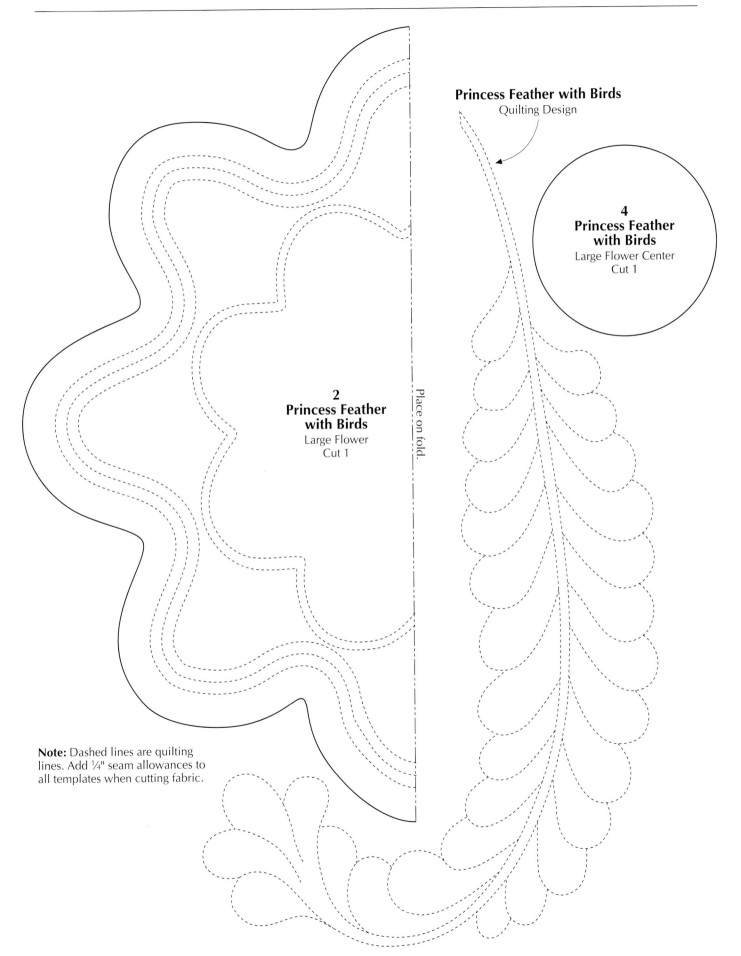

Princess Feather with Birds
Quilting Design

4
Princess Feather with Birds
Large Flower Center
Cut 1

2
Princess Feather with Birds
Large Flower
Cut 1

Place on fold

Note: Dashed lines are quilting lines. Add ¼" seam allowances to all templates when cutting fabric.

Holly Scrap Quilt II

By Deborah J. Moffett-Hall

Holly Scrap Quilt II by Deborah J. Moffett-Hall, 1994, Hatfield, Pennsylvania, 71" x 80".

DEBORAH J. MOFFETT-HALL

DEBORAH'S QUILT DESIGN CAREER BEGAN IN 1989 WHEN HER FIRST PUBLISHED PATTERN APPEARED IN *QUILT* MAGAZINE. SHE IS CURRENTLY THE SPECIAL PROJECTS EDITOR FOR *QUILT*, *COUNTRY QUILTS*, AND *OLD-FASHIONED PATCHWORK*. IN ADDITION TO HER MAGAZINE EFFORTS, DEBORAH IS NOW "HAPPILY KNEE-DEEP IN FABRIC" AS SHE SEWS QUILTS FOR HER FIRST SOLO BOOK FOR THAT PATCHWORK PLACE, TO BE PUBLISHED IN THE SPRING OF 1996.

DEBORAH LIVES IN HATFIELD, PENNSYLVANIA, WITH HER HUSBAND, SCOTT; DAUGHTER, MICHELLE; AND TRIXIE, A DOG-POUND REFUGEE WHO HAS FINALLY LEARNED TO WALK AROUND THE QUILTS SPREAD ON THE FLOOR FOR BASTING!

"HOLLY SCRAP QUILT II" EVOLVED FROM THE HOLLY QUILT DEBORAH DESIGNED FOR THE FIRST VOLUME OF *QUILTED FOR CHRISTMAS*. AS IN HER FIRST HOLLY QUILT, THE BLOCKS IN "HOLLY SCRAP QUILT II" FORM A STRONG SECONDARY PATTERN, DISGUISING THE ORIGINAL BLOCK BOUNDARIES COMPLETELY. THE DESIGN CREATES A KIND OF QUILTER'S PUZZLE: WHERE DO THE BLOCKS BEGIN AND END?

ALTHOUGH IT LOOKS COMPLEX, THIS QUILT IS SURPRISINGLY SIMPLE TO SEW, WITH ONLY FOUR PATTERN PIECES AND A BIT OF APPLIQUÉ. GOLD BUTTONS SEWN TO THE PINWHEELS GIVE THEM A CENTER TO SPIN AROUND. TO FURTHER EMPHASIZE THE SOFT SENSE OF MOTION, DEBORAH APPLIQUÉD HOLLY LEAVES IN THE WHITE "LIGHTNING BOLT" SHAPES CREATED WHEN THE BLOCKS ARE JOINED. THE QUILT IS MACHINE STIPPLE QUILTED IN THE WHITE AREAS AND TIED WITH THE BUTTONS. GOLD METALLIC THREAD HIGHLIGHTS THE HOLLY LEAVES AND BORDERS.

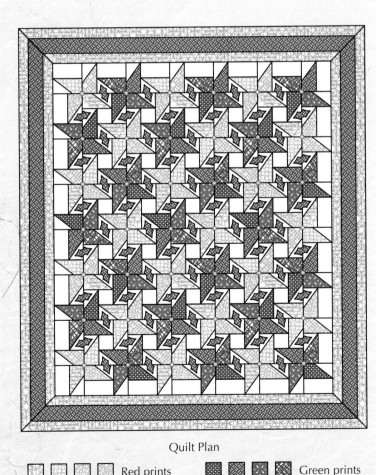

Quilt Plan

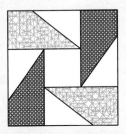

9" Block

Quilt Size: 71" x 80"
Finished Block Size: 9" x 9"

Materials: 44"-wide fabric

2 1/2 yds. red print for inner and outer border, piece A, and binding

2 1/2 yds. green print for middle border, piece A, and holly leaves

1/3 yd. each of 3 different red prints for piece A

1/3 yd. each of 3 different green prints for piece A

5/8 yd. each of 4 different white prints for pieces B, C, and D

4 2/3 yds. for backing

75" x 84" piece of batting

42 gold shank buttons, 1/2" diameter (optional)

☐ ☐ ☐ ☐ Red prints   ▨ ▨ ▨ ▨ Green prints

Cutting

Use Template A on page 35.

From the lengthwise grain of the red border print, cut:

    4 strips, each 2½" x 75", for inner and outer top and bottom borders;

    4 strips, each 2½" x 84", for inner and outer side borders;

    4 strips, each 2½" x 84", for straight-grain binding;

    2 strips, each 3½" x 84", for piece A. Cut each strip into 4 equal pieces for a total of 8 strips, each 3½" x 21". Stack 2 or 3 strips, right sides up, and cut 24 of Template A (includes 3 extra in case of errors; use 21 pieces).

Cut 24 from red border print.

From the lengthwise grain of the green border print, cut:

    2 strips, each 3½" x 75", for middle top and bottom borders;

    2 strips, each 3½" x 84", for middle side border;

    2 strips, each 3½" x 84", for piece A. Cut each strip into 4 equal pieces for a total of 8 strips, each 3½" x 21". Stack 2 or 3 strips, right sides up, and cut 24 of Template A (includes 3 extra in case of errors; use 21 pieces).

From the crosswise grain of each of the 3 red prints, cut:

    3 strips, each 3½" x 42", for a total of 9 strips; cut each strip in half to yield 18 strips, each 3½" x 21". Stack 2 or 3 strips, right sides up and edges aligned, and cut 24 of Template A from each print for a total of 72 pieces (includes 3 extra of each print in case of errors; use a total of 63 pieces).

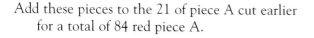

Cut 24 each from remaining three reds.

Add these pieces to the 21 of piece A cut earlier for a total of 84 red piece A.

Repeat with the 3 green prints for a total of 84 green piece A.

From the crosswise grain of each of the 4 white prints, cut:

    2 strips, each 5" x 42", for a total of 8 strips. Stack 2 or 3 strips, right sides up, and crosscut into 11 rectangles, each 3¾" x 5", to yield 88 rectangles.

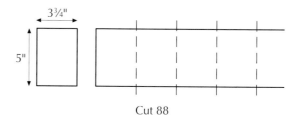

Cut 88

With right sides up, cut the rectangles diagonally in the direction shown to yield 176 triangles for piece B (includes 8 extra in case of errors; use 168 pieces).

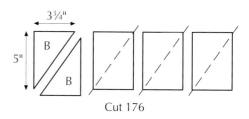

Cut 176

1 strip, each 3½" x 42", for a total of 4 strips; crosscut strips into 7 squares, each 3½" x 3½", to yield 28 squares for piece C. Cut 2 additional 3½" squares from 1 leftover strip for a total of 30 piece C. Set aside the remaining strips to cut piece D.

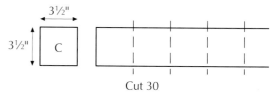

Cut 30

1 strip, each 3½" x 42", for a total of 4 strips; crosscut strips into 6 rectangles, each 3½" x 6½", to yield 24 rectangles for piece D. Cut 2 additional 3½" x 6½" rectangles from the strips left over from cutting piece C for a total of 26 piece D.

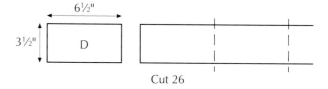

Cut 26

Piecing the Blocks
Central Blocks

1. Sew 1 white piece B to each red piece A and green piece A as shown to make 168 AB units. Press the seams toward the red and green fabrics.

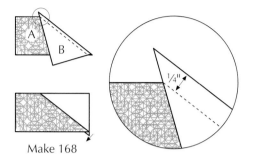

Make 168

2. Sort the AB units by color and print, assigning a number from 1–4 to each red print and 1–4 to each green print. (Note the fabrics and their numbers to avoid confusion. Consider the pieces cut from the border prints to be Red 1 and Green 1.) When assembling the blocks, use the red and green AB units with the same numbers; for example, use 2 Red 1 AB units and 2 Green 1 AB units to make 1 block.

3. With right sides together, pin 1 piece C to 1 red AB unit as shown. Stitch in the direction of the arrow, stopping ¼" from the edge of piece C. Press the seam toward the red AB unit.

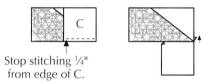

Stop stitching ¼"
from edge of C.

4. With right sides together, pin a green AB unit to the right edge of the ABC unit made in step 3. Stitch from edge to edge. Press the seam toward the green AB unit.

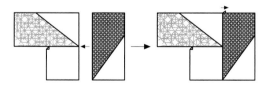

5. Continue adding AB units to piece C in a clockwise direction as shown, alternating red and green units. When you add the last green AB unit, fold the free end of the first red AB unit out of the way.

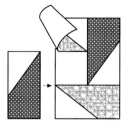

6. To complete the block, pin the first red AB unit to the last green AB unit and finish stitching the seam. Press the seam toward the red AB unit.

Finish stitching seam.

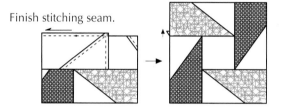

7. Using additional red and green AB units and C pieces, make:
   8 blocks using Red 1 and Green 1;
   8 blocks using Red 2 and Green 2;
   7 blocks using Red 3 and Green 3;
   7 blocks using Red 4 and Green 4.
   You should have a total of 30 blocks.

Border Blocks

1. With right sides together, pin 1 rectangle D to the lower edge of a Red 1 AB unit. Stitch. Press the seam toward the AB unit.

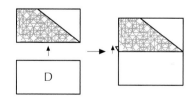

2. With right sides together, pin and stitch a Green 1 AB unit to the right edge of the ABD unit made in step 1 to complete 1 border block A. Stitch. Press the seam toward the green AB unit.

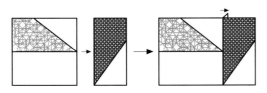

3. Using additional red and green AB units, make an additional border block A for a total of 2 blocks. Make 2 each of border blocks B, C, and D; and 7 each of border blocks E and F, for a total of 22.

Border Blocks

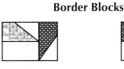

A
Make 2 using
Red 1 and Green 1.

D
Make 2 using
Green 2 and Red 2.

B
Make 2 using
Green 1 and Red 1.

E
Make 7 using
Red 3 and Green 3.

C
Make 2 using
Red 2 and Green 2.

F
Make 7 using
Green 4 and Red 4.

Corner Blocks

Pin and stitch 1 piece D to the A edge of each of the remaining 4 AB units as shown for a total of 4 corner blocks. Press the seams toward the AB units.

Corner Blocks

Upper Left Corner
Make 1 using Red 2.

Upper Right Corner
Make 1 using Green 2.

Lower Left Corner
Make 1 using Red 1.

Lower Right Corner
Make 1 using Green 1.

Assembling the Quilt Top

1. Arrange the central blocks, border blocks, and corner blocks in order by numbers and letters as shown.

Top border blocks

Left border blocks

Right border blocks

Bottom border blocks

2. Join the central blocks in horizontal rows. Press the seams in opposite directions from row to row.
3. Join the rows, making sure to match the block seams. Press the seams down.
4. Join the right and left border blocks in 2 vertical rows. Press the seams up.
5. Sew the left border row to the left side of the quilt top, making sure to match the block seams. Press the seams toward the border blocks. Repeat with the right row on the right side.
6. Join the top and bottom blocks, including the corner blocks, in two horizontal rows. Press the seams in each row in the opposite direction of the corresponding seams in the quilt top.
7. Sew the top border row to the top edge of the quilt top, making sure to match the block seams. Press the seams toward the border blocks. Repeat with the bottom row on the bottom edge.
8. Sew the border strips together as shown. Press the seams toward the red strips.

9. Attach the borders to the quilt top, following the directions for "Borders with Mitered Corners" on page 14.

Appliquéing the Holly Leaves

1. Using the Holly Leaf template below and one of the appliqué methods described on pages 9–11, prepare 71 holly leaves from the remaining green border print.
2. Arrange the leaves in the white areas created by the joined blocks. Match the dotted placement guide on each leaf to the block seam, with the tips of the holly leaf toward the points of the white area; pin in place. Appliqué the leaves.

Finishing

1. Mark the quilt top as desired or follow the quilting suggestion.

Quilting Suggestion

2. Layer the quilt top with batting and backing; baste.
3. Quilt on the marked lines. (See page 16.)
4. Bind the edges with 2½"-wide red print strips. (See pages 17–18.)
5. Sew buttons to the pinwheel centers if desired.
6. Sign your quilt. (See page 18.)

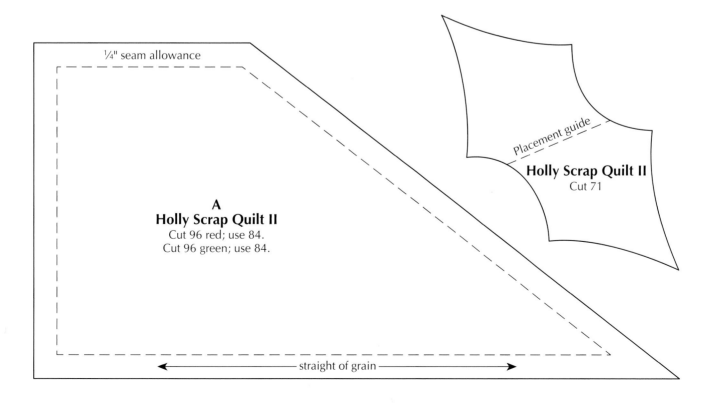

¼" seam allowance

A
Holly Scrap Quilt II
Cut 96 red; use 84.
Cut 96 green; use 84.

straight of grain

Placement guide

Holly Scrap Quilt II
Cut 71

A Victorian Christmas

By Christine Barnes

A Victorian Christmas by Christine Barnes, 1993, Grass Valley, California, 37½" x 37½".

CHRISTINE BARNES

LIKE MANY QUILTERS, CHRISTINE HAS SAMPLED A VARIETY OF QUILTING STYLES—TRADITIONAL QUILTS MADE WITH VINTAGE FABRICS, CONTEMPORARY QUILTS, MINIATURES, AND WEARABLES, TO NAME A FEW FAVORITES. IN ADDITION TO MAKING QUILTS AND SEWING CLOTHING, SHE LOVES TO PRINT AND DYE FABRIC, ESPECIALLY WITH NATURAL DYES.

CHRISTINE IS A FREE-LANCE EDITOR OF HOME DECORATING AND QUILTING BOOKS, INCLUDING SEVERAL TITLES FOR THAT PATCHWORK PLACE. OCCASIONALLY, SHE TEACHES CRAZY QUILTING AND FABRIC PAINTING. SHE LIVES IN GRASS VALLEY, A HISTORIC GOLD-MINING TOWN IN NORTHERN CALIFORNIA.

CHRISTINE WAS PICKING OUT CHRISTMAS FABRICS IN A QUILT SHOP SEVERAL YEARS AGO WHEN A WOMAN WALKED IN CARRYING A CRAZY QUILT THAT DRIPPED WITH SUMPTUOUS FABRICS, FANCY BUTTONS, AND METALLIC THREADS. SHE LOOKED AT THE BOLTS OF FABRIC IN HER ARMS, LOOKED AT THE CRAZY QUILT, AND KNEW IMMEDIATELY WHAT SHE WANTED TO MAKE.

IT TOOK SEVERAL YEARS TO COMPLETE THE WALL HANGING THAT RESULTED, AND ALONG THE WAY, CHRISTINE USED THE CRAZY QUILTING TECHNIQUE TO MAKE CHRISTMAS PILLOWS (WITH ONE BLOCK AND FOUR CORNER SQUARES) AND TABLE RUNNERS (WITH THREE BLOCKS). SHE SAYS SHE NEVER TIRES OF MAKING THESE ELEGANT BLOCKS AND EMBROIDERING THE SEAMS—EACH ONE IS DIFFERENT, LIKE A MINIATURE QUILT.

SOMEWHAT TO HER SURPRISE, CHRISTINE FOUND THAT CHILDREN LOVE LOOKING AT HER CRAZY QUILT. THEY ARE FASCINATED BY THE VICTORIAN CHARMS, ESPECIALLY THE SMALL HARE LEAPING OVER THE DEER IN THE LEFT MIDDLE BLOCK AND THE SEAHORSE IN THE LOWER RIGHT BLOCK.

Quilt Plan

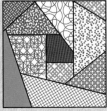

9½" Block
Spiraling

9½" Block
Radiating

Quilt Size: 37½" x 37½"
Finished Block Size: 9½" x 9½"

Materials: 44"-wide fabric

1¼ yds. muslin for foundation squares

⅛ yd. black moiré for blocks

¼ yd. each of 8 Christmas prints
for blocks and corner squares

¼ yd. each of 4 Christmas plaids
for blocks and corner squares

¼ yd. each of green satin and
green cotton velveteen for blocks

¼ yd. each of red satin and
red cotton velveteen for blocks

¼ yd. gold brocade for blocks

1½ yds. green moiré for borders and binding

1½ yds. Christmas print for backing and rod sleeve

Gold metallic thread, rayon floss, and ribbon floss

Embroidery needle

18 Victorian charms

Cutting

From the muslin, cut:
> 9 squares, each 11" x 11", for block foundations;
> 4 squares, each 5¹/₂" x 5¹/₂", for corner square foundations.

From the black moiré, cut:
> 3 squares, each 3" x 3", for centers of spiraling blocks.

From a red Christmas print, cut:
> 1 square, 3" x 3", for center of spiraling block.

From the green satin, cut:
> 1 square, 3" x 3", for center of spiraling block.

From the green moiré, cut:
> 4 strips, each 5" x 42", for borders*;
> 4 strips, each 2" x 42", for binding.

From the prints, plaids, velveteens, and brocade, cut pieces as you work, as directed below.

*Cut 2 strips on the crosswise grain and 2 strips on the lengthwise grain.

Making the Blocks
Spiraling Blocks

In this method, you begin with a center square and add pieces in a clockwise direction. The following instructions are for the lower left block in the quilt. Cut the required pieces from the assorted remaining fabrics as desired.

1. Trim 1 corner on a 3" center square to make piece 1. Center piece 1 on an 11" muslin foundation square, placing the angled edge at the upper right; pin.

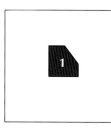

2. For piece 2, cut a 3¹/₂" square from your choice of the remaining fabrics.
3. Lay piece 2 on piece 1, with right sides together, aligning the raw edges at the lower edge of piece 1; pin. Stitch, using a ¹/₈"-wide seam allowance.

Flip piece 2 right side up and press. Using your rotary ruler and chalk, draw a line extending from the left edge of piece 1 across piece 2. This line is your guide for placing and stitching piece 3.

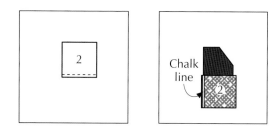

4. For piece 3, cut a rectangle 4" x 6³/₄", or slightly longer than the left edge of piece 1 and the chalk line.
5. Lay piece 3 on pieces 1 and 2, with right sides together. Align the raw edge of piece 3 with the left edge of piece 1 and the chalk line; pin. Stitch.

   Flip piece 3 right side up and press. Draw a chalk line extending from the upper edge of piece 1 across piece 3.

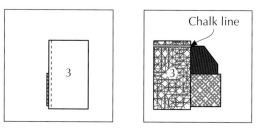

6. For piece 4, cut a rectangle 4" x 5¹/₂", or slightly longer than the upper edge of piece 1 and the chalk line.
7. Lay piece 4 on pieces 1 and 3, with right sides together. Align the raw edge of piece 4 with the upper edge of piece 1 and the chalk line; pin. Stitch.

   Flip piece 4 right side up and press. Draw a chalk line extending from the angled edge of piece 1 across piece 4.

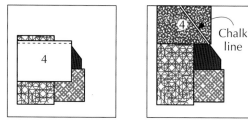

8. For piece 5, cut a rectangle 4" x 8½", or slightly longer than the angled edge of piece 1 and the chalk line. Pin, stitch, and flip piece 5 as you did the previous pieces. Trim the excess fabric from piece 4. You may need to remove some stitching on piece 4 to lift and trim it. After you flip piece 5, trim it even with the upper edge of the foundation square.

Draw chalk lines extending from the right edge of piece 1 across pieces 2 and 5.

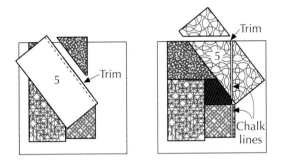

9. For piece 6, cut a rectangle 4" x 10½", or slightly longer than the right edge of piece 1 and the chalk lines. Pin, stitch, and flip piece 6. Trim the excess fabric from piece 5.

Draw a diagonal chalk line from the right edge to the lower edge of the foundation square through pieces 2 and 6.

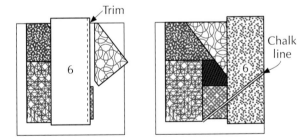

10. For piece 7, cut a rectangle 6" wide and slightly longer than the chalk line. Pin, stitch, and flip piece 7. Trim the excess fabric from pieces 2 and 6. Trim piece 7 even with the edges of the foundation square.

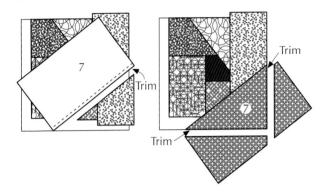

11. Add pieces 8–11 one at a time, first drawing an angled chalk line as a guide. Avoid drawing lines that are parallel to the seams. Be sure to cut each piece wide enough and long enough to cover the foundation. Trim the excess fabric from the pieces as you work. Finally, trim the pieces even with the edges of the foundation square. Baste close to the edges of the completed square.

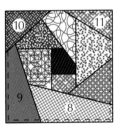

12. Make 4 more spiraling blocks. For slightly different block designs, trim 2 or more corners from the center square and vary the angles of the pieces.

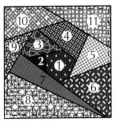

Design Tips for Crazy Quilters

For the delightfully jumbled look that typifies Crazy quilts, follow these guidelines:

- Contrast is very important in a Crazy quilt. Alternate red and green, print and solid, smooth and napped, and light and dark fabrics for a balanced look. When choosing fabrics for adjacent pieces, squint; if the pieces blend, there's not enough contrast. It's easier to achieve contrast if you have approximately the same number of red and green fabrics.
- Slight differences in the sizes and shapes of the first pieces will alter the sizes of the following pieces. Before you cut each piece, roughly measure the area to make sure your piece will be large enough. A common—and frustrating—mistake is to cut pieces that are too small.
- As you make blocks and develop an eye for shapes, you'll see how to use the trimmed pieces in other blocks.

Radiating Blocks

In this method, you add the pieces to the foundation square in an arc, beginning at one corner. The following instructions are for the upper middle block in the quilt. Cut the required pieces from the assorted remaining fabrics as desired.

1. From a print or solid, cut a 4" x 4½" piece; trim 2 adjacent corners to make piece 1. Position this piece in the lower left corner of an 11" muslin foundation square, with the angled edges toward the center; pin.

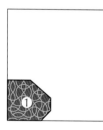

2. For piece 2, cut a 3½" square from your choice of the remaining fabrics.

3. Lay piece 2 on piece 1, right sides together, aligning the raw edges at the upper edge of piece 1; pin. Stitch, using a ⅛"-wide seam allowance.

   Flip piece 2 right side up and press. Draw a chalk line extending from the upper angled edge of piece 1 across piece 2.

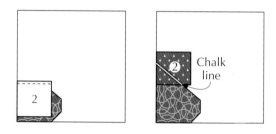

4. For piece 3, cut a rectangle 3½" wide and 1" longer than the angled edge of piece 1 and the chalk line on piece 2.

5. Lay piece 3 on pieces 1 and 2, right sides together, aligning the raw edge of piece 3 with the edge of piece 1 and the chalk line. Allow the extra length of piece 3 to extend beyond the left edge of the foundation square; pin. Stitch.

   Flip piece 3 right side up and press. Trim the excess fabric from piece 2. Trim piece 3 even with the left edge of the foundation square. Draw a chalk line extending from the right edge of piece 1 (the shortest edge) across piece 3.

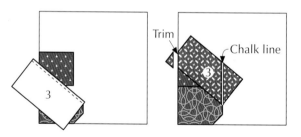

6. For piece 4, cut a rectangle 3" wide and 1" longer than the edge of piece 1 and the chalk line. Pin, stitch, and flip piece 4 as you did the previous pieces. Trim the excess fabric from piece 3.

7. Repeat with piece 5. Trim piece 5 even with the lower edge of the foundation square.

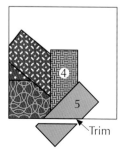

8. Reverse the direction and add piece 6 to the edges of pieces 4 and 5. Add pieces 7 and 8 as you did the previous pieces. Add piece 9 to the right edge and piece 10 to the upper right corner. Trim the excess fabric from each piece as you work. Baste close to the edges of the completed square.

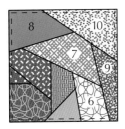

9. Make 3 more radiating blocks. For slightly different block designs, vary the angles of the pieces.

Corner Squares

You'll need 4 small corner squares for the borders. The instructions that follow are for the upper left corner square.

1. Cut and pin piece 1 to the lower left corner of a 5½" foundation square.
2. Cut piece 2 slightly longer than the edge of piece 1. Lay piece 2 on piece 1, right sides together, aligning the raw edges; pin. Stitch. Flip piece 2 right side up and press.
3. Pin, stitch, and flip pieces 3 and 4. Trim the excess fabric even with the edges of the foundation square.
4. Baste close to the edges of the square.

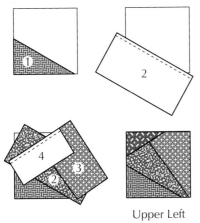

Upper Left
Corner Square

5. Make 3 more corner squares, using the numbered illustrations below as a guide.

Upper Right Corner Square   Lower Left Corner Square   Lower Right Corner Square

Assembling the Quilt Top

1. On each spiraling and radiating square, measure and mark a 10" block. On each corner square, measure and mark a 5" square. Baste just inside the marked perimeter; trim each block and corner square on the marked lines.
2. Arrange the 10" blocks in 3 rows of 3 blocks each as shown in the quilt plan, placing the spiraling blocks in the center and corners, and the radiating blocks in the remaining positions. Rotate the blocks for variety. If possible, don't allow pieces of the same fabric to touch where blocks join.
3. Sew the blocks together in horizontal rows. Press the seams in opposite directions from row to row. Join the rows, making sure to match the seams.
4. Embroider the seams that join the blocks, referring to "Embroidery Stitches" on the following page.

Finishing

1. Attach the borders, following the directions on page 13 for "Borders with Corner Squares" but disregarding the references to piecing the borders or cutting corner squares. Attach the borders so the grain line on the moiré runs in the same direction.
2. Embroider the seams that join the border and corner squares to the blocks.
3. Layer the quilt top with backing; baste.
4. Bind the edges with the green moiré strips. (See pages 17–18.) Cut the strips 2" wide for a narrow binding.
5. Sew the Victorian charms to the blocks.
6. Sign your quilt. (See page 18.)

Embroidery Stitches

Embellish the seams of your Crazy quilt blocks and corner squares with decorative embroidery stitches. Below are the four stitches used on the quilt, but you can add as many different stitches as you like. Be sure to vary the threads and stitches from block to block.

The *feather stitch* consists of a series of alternating loops worked from the top to the bottom. The key to making a consistent feather stitch is to insert the needle (D) directly opposite the point where the needle emerged (C).

Feather Stitch

The *cross-stitch* accentuates seams. Like the feather stitch, this stitch is worked over the seam.

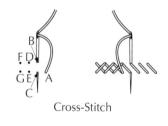

Cross-Stitch

The *cretan stitch*, one of the fastest embroidery stitches to do, is worked over the seam. This stitch decorates the seams joining the blocks and the border.

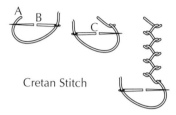

Cretan Stitch

The *chain stitch* outlines seams. For extra emphasis, use ribbon floss.

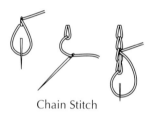

Chain Stitch

Christmas Seminole

By Nadine Rogeret

Christmas Seminole by Nadine Rogeret, 1994, Normandie, France, 76" x 76".

NADINE ROGERET

NADINE ROGERET IS A WELL-KNOWN NAME TO QUILTERS AROUND THE WORLD, AND PARTICULARLY TO FRENCH QUILTERS. IT IS AN HONOR TO FEATURE HER WORK IN THIS BOOK. BORN IN LE HAVRE, FRANCE, NADINE GREW UP WANTING TO BECOME A DECORATOR. SHE DISCOVERED QUILTMAKING IN 1977 AT THE MAISON DES METIERS IN BOURNEVILLE, FRANCE, AND FOUND IT TO BE A NATURAL MEDIUM FOR EXPRESSING HERSELF IN A RELATED ART. BY 1984, NADINE HAD OPENED HER OWN QUILT STUDIO/SHOP IN LE HAVRE. HER WORK HAS APPEARED IN MAGAZINES AND IN SEVERAL LARGE SHOWS, INCLUDING A SHOW AT THE LE HAVRE CHAMBER OF COMMERCE IN 1987, WHERE SHE HUNG SIXTY-THREE LARGE QUILTS, AND IN THE 1989 SHOW, "THE FINE ART OF QUILTING," WHERE SHE WAS CITED AS "ONE OF THE WORLD'S FORTY-EIGHT BEST QUILTERS."

SINCE ITS OPENING, NADINE'S SHOP HAS DOUBLED IN SIZE, AND IN 1991 SHE OPENED THE FIRST MUSEUM OF PATCHWORK AND COURETEPOINT IN PARTNERSHIP WITH THE PARC NATUREL REGIONAL DE BROTONNE. SHE CONTINUES TO SHOW HER WORK IN FRANCE AND THROUGHOUT EUROPE AND HAS PARTICIPATED IN QUILT EUROPA AND THE INTERNATIONAL QUILT FESTIVAL IN HOUSTON.

AMERICAN QUILTMAKING TECHNIQUES, SUCH AS SEMINOLE PATCHWORK, ARE OF GREAT INTEREST TO NADINE, WHO ENJOYS TEACHING THEM IN HER CLASSES. SHE DESIGNED THIS QUILT AROUND A COLLECTION OF CHRISTMAS FABRICS DESIGNED BY JINNY BEYER AS A WAY TO USE HER FAVORITE COLORS AND EXPRESS A MORE CONTEMPORARY APPROACH TO SEMINOLE PIECING.

STRIPS CUT FROM A BEAUTIFUL BORDER PRINT FRAME THE EDGES OF THIS QUILT AS WELL AS THE BLOCKS IN THE CENTER MEDALLION, WHILE THREE DIFFERENT VERSIONS OF SEMINOLE PATCHWORK DRAW THE EYE AROUND THE CENTER AND CORNER BLOCKS.

EDITOR'S NOTE: BECAUSE THIS QUILT COMES FROM FRANCE, IT WAS DESIGNED AND DRAFTED USING THE METRIC MEASUREMENT SYSTEM. WHEN THE PATTERN WAS TRANSLATED TO INCHES FOR AMERICAN QUILTERS, THE MEASUREMENTS CHANGED, SO THE QUILT YOU SEE IN THE QUILT PLAN DIFFERS SOMEWHAT FROM THE QUILT SHOWN IN THE PHOTO. THE OVERALL EFFECT, HOWEVER, WILL BE THE SAME.

Quilt Plan

Quilt Size: 76" x 76"

Materials: 44"-wide fabric

2½ yds. border print for outer border and sashing

¾ yd. poinsettia or other Christmas print for medallion blocks

1¾ yds. subtle red print or solid for medallion border and outer corner blocks

1⅛ yds. subtle green print or solid for large triangles and medallion center square

1⅛ yds. dark green solid for Seminole piecing

2 yds. subtle gray print for center medallion blocks

¾ yd. red solid for Seminole piecing

⅜ yd. each of 5 different greens for Seminole piecing in outer corner blocks

⅝ yd. red solid for binding

4¼ yds. fabric for backing

80" x 80" piece of batting

Note: It is a good idea to choose the border print first, then choose the other fabrics to coordinate with it. The border print should have at least 2 different design areas, one that you can cut into 5¼"-wide strips for the outer border and another that you can cut into 5½"-wide strips for the sashing between the medallion blocks. Border designs or striped designs are normally printed along the length of the fabric. If a border print is not available, consider a Christmas plaid, stripe, or print for the borders instead. If it is not necessary to cut the strips along the length of the fabric, you will need less fabric.

Block A   Block B   Block C

Cutting

Cut the pieces listed below first, then set aside the remaining fabrics for the Seminole piecing.

From the border print, cut:
    8 strips, each 5¼" x 42", for outer border;
    4 strips, each 5½" x 21½", for medallion sashing.
From the poinsettia print, cut:
    4 squares, each 11½" x 11½", for Blocks A and B.
From the subtle red print, cut:
    4 strips, each 4" x 56", for center medallion
        borders;
    4 squares, each 9½" x 9½", for outer corners,
        Block C.
From the subtle green print, cut:
    1 square, 5½" x 5½", for center square;
    4 squares, each 15¼" x 15¼"; cut once diagonally
        for 8 large setting triangles for outer corners.

Christmas Cross Seminole Strips
Cutting
Cut the strips listed below, setting them aside in piles for Strip Unit 1 and Strip Unit 2. Cut all strips across the fabric width. If your fabric is not at least 40" wide, you may need to cut additional strips for Strip Unit 2. Do not do so until you have assembled those shown below and cut them into segments as directed to determine if you need an additional strip unit.

From the dark green solid, cut:
    4 strips, each 1¼" x 42", for Strip Unit 1;
    3 strips, each 1¼" x 42", for Strip Unit 2.
From the subtle gray print, cut:
    4 strips, each 1¾" x 42", for Strip Unit 1;
    3 strips, each 3¼" x 42", for Strip Unit 2;
    3 strips, each 1¾" x 42", for Strip Unit 2.
From the red solid, cut:
    2 strips each 1¼" x 42", for Strip Unit 1.

Assembly
1. For Strip Unit 1, sew the strips together as shown. Press the seams in the direction of the arrows. Make 2 identical strip units. Cut a total of 48 segment 1, each 1¼" wide, from the completed units.

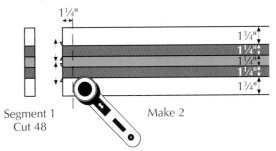

Segment 1
Cut 48   Make 2

2. For Strip Unit 2, sew the strips together as shown. Press the seams in the direction of the arrows. Make 3 identical strip units. Cut a total of 96 segment 2, each 1¼" wide, from the completed units.

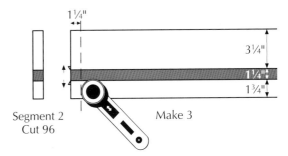

Segment 2
Cut 96   Make 3

3. Sew 2 of segment 2 to each of 24 segment 1, offsetting as shown so that the seam lines of the green squares match those of the red square in each resulting unit. Press the seams toward segment 2.

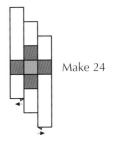

Make 24

4. Repeat with the remaining segment 1 and 2 pieces, offsetting in the opposite direction as shown. Press the seams toward segment 2.

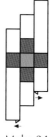

Make 24

5. Arrange the resulting units into groups of 5 and 7. Sew the units together, offsetting as shown and being very careful to stitch an accurate 1/4"-wide seam. Check the resulting strip width. Each one should measure 3/4" from seam line to seam line. Adjust stitching if necessary. Press.

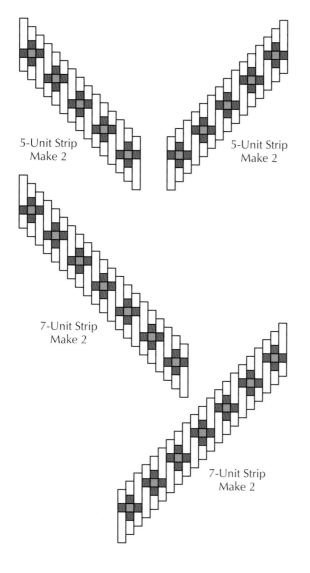

5-Unit Strip
Make 2

5-Unit Strip
Make 2

7-Unit Strip
Make 2

7-Unit Strip
Make 2

6. Using rotary-cutting equipment, measure and mark trim lines on each strip 1/2" from the points of the green squares as shown. The resulting strips should be 3 1/2" wide. Trim the strips. The long edges of these strips are on the bias, so handle them carefully to prevent stretching.

3 1/2"

Trim 1/2" from points of green squares.

7. From the dark green solid, cut 2 strips, each 1 1/2" x 42". Crosscut into 4 strips, each 1 1/2" x 15 3/8". Pin and sew a green strip to the bottom edge of each 5-unit strip. Trim even with the 45°-angle edge and trim the remaining end at a 90° angle to the long edge so that it measures 11 5/8" as shown. You should have 2 sets of mirror-image units. Set aside for center medallion blocks.

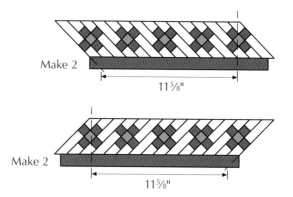

Make 2

11 5/8"

Make 2

11 5/8"

8. From the gray print, cut 4 strips, each 3 1/2" x 21 3/8". Sew a gray strip to the bottom edge of each 7-unit strip. Trim as shown. You should have 2 sets of mirror-image units. Set aside for center medallion blocks.

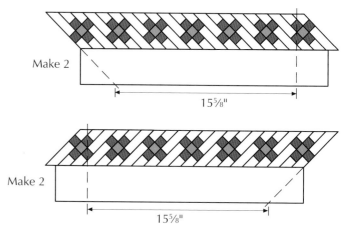

Make 2

15 5/8"

Make 2

15 5/8"

Diamond Seminole Strips

Cutting

Cut all strips across the fabric width.

From the red solid, cut:
  6 strips, each 2¼" x 42".
From the subtle gray print, cut:
  6 strips, each 1¼" x 42".
From the dark green solid, cut:
  6 strips, each 2¼" x 42".

Assembly

Note: Because you will be working with many bias segments to make the required strip units for this patchwork, it is extremely important to make all cuts
  carefully and to stitch accurate ¼"-wide seams.

1. Sew the strips together as shown and press the seams
   toward the red strip. You will need to make a mini-
   mum of 6 identical strip units. If your fabric is not
   at least 40" wide after preshrinking or if you must
   do many cleanup cuts (see Note in next column) to
   keep the cut edges of the segments on the true bias,
   you may need to make another strip unit.

2. Layer 2 strips with right sides facing and make a
   45°-angle cut at one end. Repeat with the remaining strips.

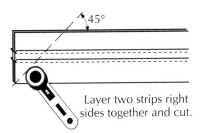

Layer two strips right
sides together and cut.

3. With the ruler parallel to the angled cut edge, cut
   segments 1¼" wide from each unit. You will need a
   total of 72 segments that slant up to the left and 72
   segments that slant up to the right.

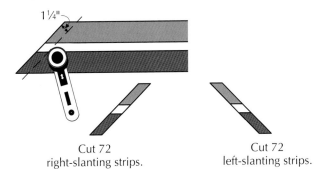

Cut 72
right-slanting strips.

Cut 72
left-slanting strips.

Note: After cutting every second or third strip, check
  the angle of the cut edge of the strip unit to make
  sure it is an exact 45° angle. Re-cut as needed before proceeding to cut the next segments. With this
  type of piecing, the slightest cutting discrepancies
  can drastically affect the final size.

4. Sew 15 of the right-slanting segments together, offsetting each strip as shown. It is easier to sew the
   segments together into 7 pairs, then sew the pairs
   together, and finally add 1 more segment. Press all
   seams in one direction after joining all units. Before pressing, check to make sure that the strips
   measure ¾" from seam line to seam line. Adjust
   stitching if necessary. Repeat to make 1 more unit
   with 15 right-slanting segments, and 2 units with
   21 left-slanting segments.

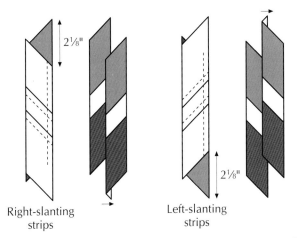

Right-slanting
strips

Left-slanting
strips

5. Using rotary-cutting equipment, measure and mark
   trim lines on each strip ⅞" from the points of the
   gray diamonds as shown. The resulting strips should
   be 3½" wide. As you position your rotary ruler for
   cutting, make sure to keep the 45°-angle line on

the ruler aligned with an angled edge or seam line to ensure finished strips that are the correct width and shape. Trim the strips.

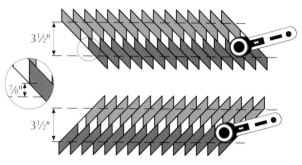

6. From the gray print, cut 2 strips, each 1½" x 42". Crosscut into 4 strips, each 1½" x 15⅜". Pin and sew a gray strip to the bottom edge of each 15-segment strip. Trim even with the 45°-angle edge and trim the remaining end at a 90° angle to the long edge so that it measures 11⅝" as shown. You should have 2 sets of mirror-image units. Set aside for the center medallion blocks.

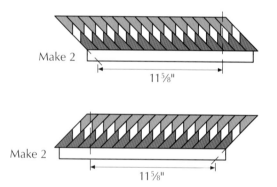

Make 2

11⅝"

Make 2

11⅝"

7. From the gray print, cut 4 strips, each 3½" x 21⅜". Sew a gray strip to the bottom edge of each 21-segment strip. Trim as shown. You should have 2 sets of mirror-image units. Set aside for the center medallion blocks.

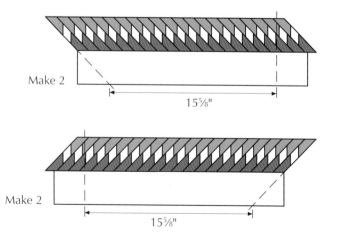

Make 2

15⅝"

Make 2

15⅝"

Multi-Square Seminole Strips

Cutting

Before you begin, arrange the 5 greens you have chosen in the desired order and number them 1–5. Cut all strips across the fabric width.

From green 1, cut:
  4 strips, each 2¾" x 42".
From green 2, cut:
  4 strips, each 1½" x 42".
From green 3, cut:
  4 strips, each 1½" x 42".
From green 4, cut:
  4 strips, each 1½" x 42".
From green 5, cut:
  4 strips, each 2¾" x 42".

Assembly

1. Sew the strips together to make 4 identical strip-pieced units. Press the seams in one direction in 2 of the strip units and in the opposite direction in the remaining pair. Cut 1½"-wide segments from the resulting units. You will need a total of 88 segments. Divide the segments into 2 groups of an equal number.

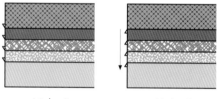

Make 2   Make 2

Press seams in opposite directions
in each pair of strip units.

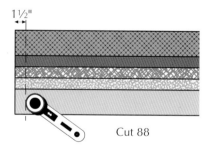

1½"

Cut 88

2. Working with one group of the segments, make 4 units containing 11 segments each; sew them together stair-step fashion as shown, making sure that the seam allowances butt at each intersection.

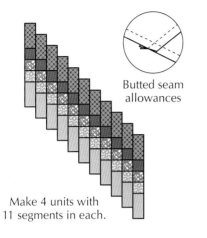

Butted seam allowances

Make 4 units with 11 segments in each.

3. Repeat step 2, working with the remaining group of segments and stair-stepping them in the opposite direction.

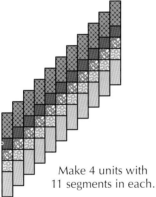

Make 4 units with 11 segments in each.

4. Align the 45° line on the rotary ruler with one of the long seams in a unit and trim so that the design is centered and the resulting strip is 4½" wide. Repeat with all remaining units.

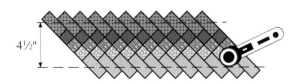

4½"

5. From the dark green solid, cut 4 strips, each 1⅞" x 42". Crosscut a total of 8 strips, each 1⅞" x 16½". Stitch one to the bottom edge of each strip unit and trim as shown.

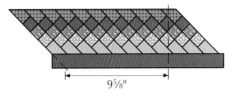

9⅝"

Assembling the Quilt
Center Blocks A and B

1. Arrange the Christmas Cross Seminole strips in pairs as shown. Repeat with the Diamond Seminole strips and the Multi-Square Seminole strips.

Christmas Cross Seminole

Diamond Seminole

Multi-Square Seminole

2. Join the pairs along the angled edges, beginning at the seam intersection at the inner corner and making sure that the seam allowances match. Set the Multi-Square Seminole strips aside for the corner blocks (Block C).

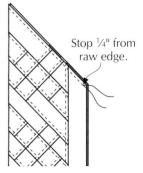

Stop ¼" from raw edge.

3. Sew a short Christmas Cross mitered border to 2 of the poinsettia squares as shown. Begin stitching at the inner corner of the miter and stitch to the outer edge of the square. Backstitch at the beginning to secure. Repeat, using the short Diamond mitered borders and the 2 remaining poinsettia squares.

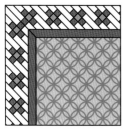 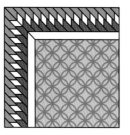

Center Block A   Center Block B

4. Sew the long mitered borders to each of the squares as shown, stitching in the same manner as you did to add the short borders.

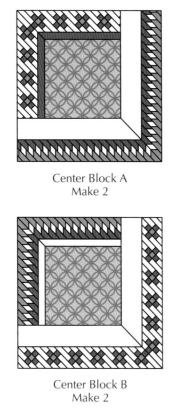

Center Block A
Make 2

Center Block B
Make 2

5. Arrange the completed center blocks with the sashing strips and the center square as shown, paying careful attention to the position of each block.

Sew together in rows; press the seams toward the sashing strips. Join the rows; press the seams toward the sashing strips.

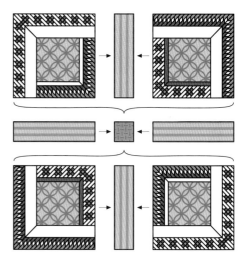

6. Attach the red print border strips to the center medallion, mitering corners as shown on page 14. The finished piece should measure 54½" x 54½". Set the completed medallion center aside.

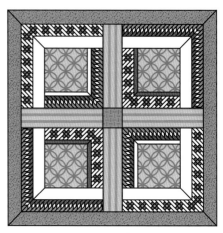

Corner Blocks

1. Sew a mitered Multi-Square Seminole border to each of the 4 red corner squares.

Corner Block
Make 4

2. Sew a large green triangle to each side of the block as shown. Press the seams toward the triangles.

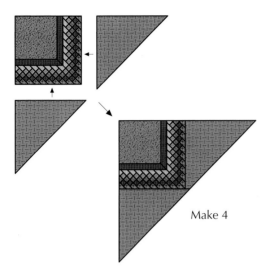

Make 4

3. Add mitered borders to the resulting triangle. Press the seams toward the borders. The border strips will extend beyond each end of the triangle. Trim even with the bottom edge.

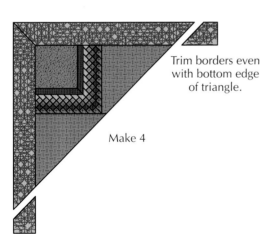

Trim borders even with bottom edge of triangle.

Make 4

4. Sew triangles to the sides of the center medallion.

Finishing

1. Mark the quilt top as desired.
2. Layer the quilt top with batting and backing; baste.
3. Quilt on the marked lines. (See page 16.)
4. Bind the edges with 2¹/₂"-wide red straight-grain strips. (See pages 17–18).
5. Sign your quilt. (See page 18.)

Cardinals in the Forest

By Mary Ellen Von Holt

Cardinals in the Forest by Mary Ellen Von Holt, 1994, Marietta, Georgia, 58$\frac{1}{2}$" x 35$\frac{3}{4}$".

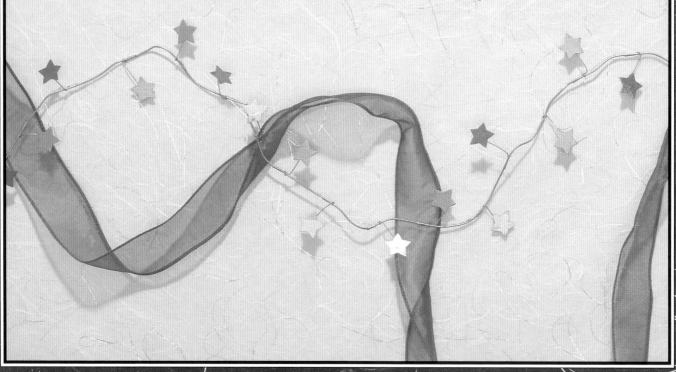

MARY ELLEN VON HOLT

MARY ELLEN HAS BEEN QUILTING FOR MORE THAN FIFTEEN YEARS AND LOVES ALL PHASES OF QUILTMAKING. SHE AND PARTNERS ALICE BERG AND SYLVIA JOHNSON COMBINE THEIR TALENTS TO PRODUCE LITTLE QUILTS PATTERNS, KITS, AND ACCESSORIES, WHICH ARE SOLD WORLDWIDE. LITTLE QUILTS RECENTLY ADDED A LINE OF FABRICS TO ITS COLLECTION.

AS A QUILT DESIGNER AND QUILTMAKER, MARY ELLEN PUTS HER ART AND ADVERTISING BACKGROUND TO GOOD USE. CHALLENGE PROJECTS AND WALL HANGINGS ARE HER SPECIALTIES, AND SHE IS KNOWN FOR HER SKILL IN FABRIC COORDINATION. SHE TEACHES CLASSES IN MAKING TRADITIONAL SCRAP QUILTS AND HAS JUST ADDED PRIMITIVE-STYLE RUG HOOKING TO HER REPERTOIRE.

WHEN MARY ELLEN SAW THESE ANTIQUE TREE BLOCKS AT A QUILT SHOW IN 1993, THE SMALL RED TRIANGLES BROUGHT TO MIND "CARDINALS IN THE TREE." AT THE TIME, SHE WANTED TO MAKE A CHRISTMAS WALL HANGING FOR HER DINING ROOM, SO SHE BOUGHT THE BLOCKS (WHICH WERE ALREADY JOINED TO THE BLACK SETTING TRIANGLES) AND FRAMED THEM WITH INNER AND OUTER BORDERS. WHAT THE QUILT NEEDED, OF COURSE, WERE MORE CARDINALS! APPLIQUÉD BIRDS CUT FROM SCRAPPY RED PRINTS OVERLOOK THE SCENE, AND ASSORTED STARS AND MOONS SET A NIGHTTIME MOOD.

Quilt Plan

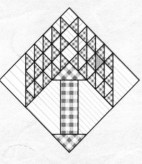

16" Block

Quilt Size: 58½" x 35¾"
Finished Tree Block Size: 16" x 16"

Materials: 44"-wide fabric

½ yd. black-and-white check for treetops

¾ yd. light print, such as a reproduction shirting or haberdashery fabric, for tree background

1 red print scrap, at least 3" x 3", for 2 "cardinal" triangles in treetops

1 fat quarter (18" x 22") larger black-and-white check for tree trunks

1 yd. black solid for background

¼ yd. green print for inner border

17 assorted gold and white print scraps, at least 5" x 5", for stars and moons

9 assorted red scraps, at least 5" x 8", for birds

1 fat quarter (18" x 22") green print for stems

1½ yds. gold homespun for outer border

1 yd. paper-backed fusible web

1¾ yds. for backing

40" x 60" piece of thin batting

½ yd. black print for binding

Black embroidery floss

Cutting

Use templates on pages 56–57.

From the black-and-white check, cut:
    1 piece, 12" x 42", for bias squares;
    7 squares, each 2⅞" x 2⅞"; cut once diagonally
        to yield 14 half-square triangles for piece B.

From the light print, cut:
    1 piece, 12" x 42", for bias squares;
    6 squares, each 2½" x 2½", for background
        piece A;
    2 squares, each 6⅞" x 6⅞"; cut once diagonally
        to yield 4 half-square triangles for background
        piece D;
    4 of Template F for background.

From the 3" x 3" red print scrap, cut:
    1 square, 2⅞" x 2⅞"; cut once diagonally for
        contrast piece B.

From the larger black-and-white check, cut:
    2 rectangles, each 3⅜" x 9", for piece E;
    2 squares, each 4⅞" x 4⅞"; cut once diagonally
        to yield 4 half-square triangles for piece C.

From the black solid, cut:
    2 squares, each 12⅛" x 12⅛"; cut once diagonally
        to yield 4 half-square corner setting triangles;
    1 square, 16⅞" x 16⅞"; cut once diagonally
        to yield 2 half-square middle setting triangles.

From the green print, cut:
    4 strips, each 1½" x 42", for inner border.

From the gold and white scraps, cut:
    6 of Template 1 for large stars;
    7 of Template 2 for small stars;
    4 of Template 3 for moons.

From the assorted red scraps, cut:
    4 of Template 4, and 5 of Template 4 reversed, for
        birds.

From the green print, cut:
    4 of Template 5, and 4 of Template 5 reversed, for
        stems.

From the lengthwise grain of the gold homespun, cut:
    4 strips, each 5¾" x 54", for outer border.

Piecing the Tree Blocks

1. Pair the 12" x 42" black-and-white and light print fabrics. Following the directions for "Making Bias Squares" on pages 7–8, cut bias strips 2½" wide, strip-pieced segments 2½" wide, and bias squares 2½" x 2½". You will need a total of 46 bias squares.

2. Sew 1 small checked triangle to 1 red scrap triangle to make 1 pieced square. Press the seam toward the darker fabric and trim the "dog-ear" corners. Make 2 red-and-checked pieced squares.

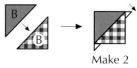

3. Sew 9 pieced squares (including 1 red-and-checked square) and 3 light triangles in rows as shown. Press the seams open. Join the rows to make 1 unit.

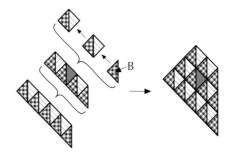

Make a second unit that is the mirror image of the first, but without the red-and-checked square.

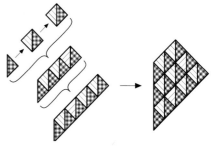

4. Sew 6 pieced squares and 3 light squares, each 2½" x 2½", in rows as shown. Press the seams open. Join the rows to make 1 unit.

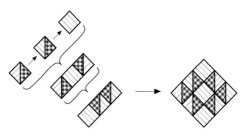

5. Sew piece D to the side of a unit made in step 3 as shown. Press the seam toward piece D. Make a second unit that is the mirror image of the first.

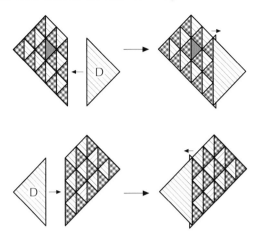

6. Sew piece F to each side of piece E. Press the seams toward piece F. Sew piece C to the top and bottom of the unit. Press the seams toward piece C.

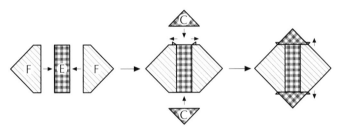

7. Sew the units together in rows as shown. Press the seams in opposite directions. Join the rows to make 1 Tree block.

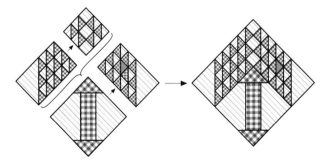

8. Make a second block, changing the placement of the small red triangle as shown in the quilt photo and plan.

Assembling the Quilt Top and Finishing

1. Press the Tree blocks. Each block should measure 16½" x 16½", including seam allowances.
2. Arrange the blocks and setting triangles as shown. Sew a middle setting triangle to each Tree block. (Be careful not to stretch the long bias edges on these triangles.) Press the seams toward the triangles. Sew the blocks together diagonally. Sew the corner setting triangles to the blocks. Press the seams toward the triangles.

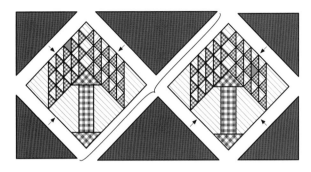

3. Sew the inner border to the quilt top, following the directions for "Straight-Cut Borders" on page 13, with this important change: stitch the top and bottom border strips first, then the side strips.
4. Using paper-backed fusible web, prepare the star, moon, and bird appliqué pieces. Follow the manufacturer's directions carefully. No seam allowances are needed when using this method.
5. Arrange the stars, moons, and birds as shown in the quilt plan on page 53. Fuse in place. Using black embroidery floss and a buttonhole or blanket stitch, finish the edges.

Buttonhole Stitch

6. Sew the outer border to the quilt top in the same order as the inner border.
7. Appliqué the remaining birds and the stems to the outer border.

8. Mark the quilt top as desired or follow the quilting suggestion.

9. Layer the quilt top with batting and backing; baste.

10. Quilt on the marked lines. (See page 16.)

11. Bind the edges with 2½"-wide black straight-grain strips. (See pages 17–18.)

12. Sign your quilt. (See page 18.)

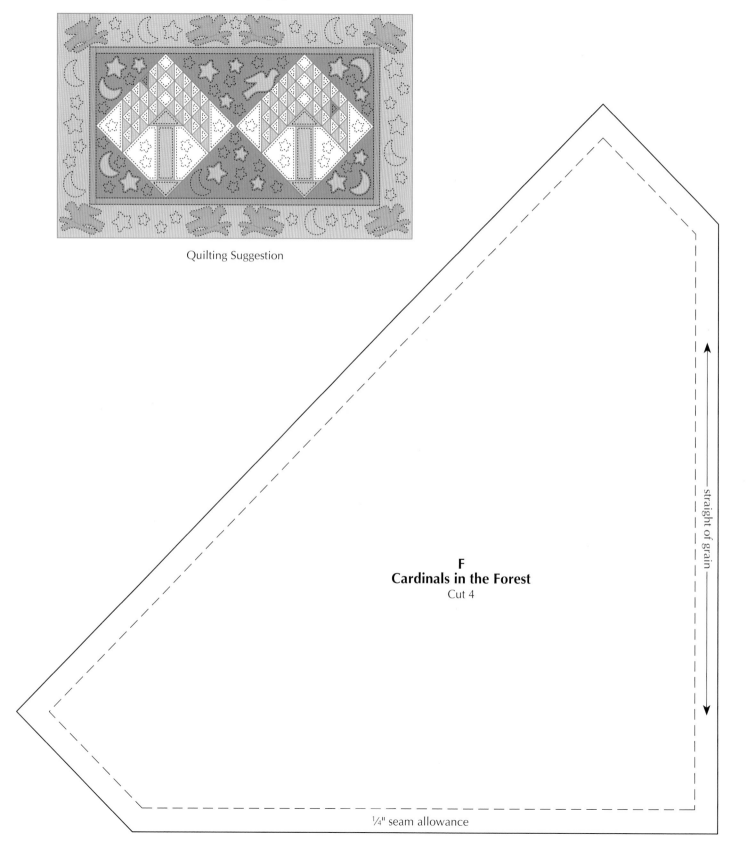

Quilting Suggestion

F
Cardinals in the Forest
Cut 4

straight of grain

¼" seam allowance

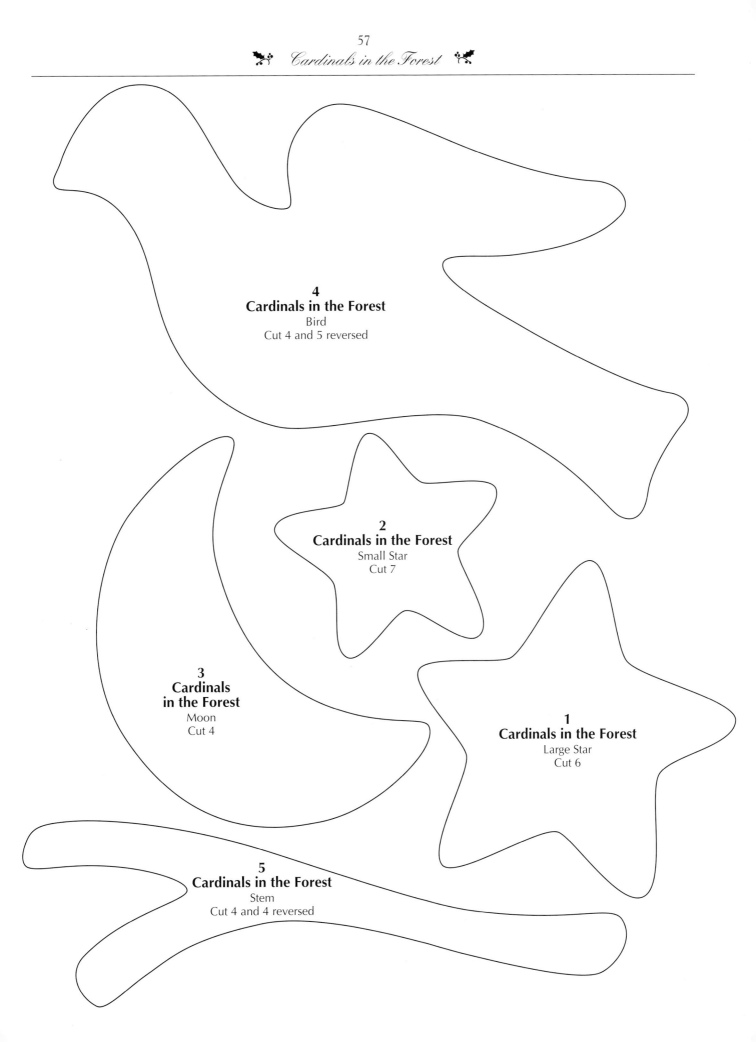

4
Cardinals in the Forest
Bird
Cut 4 and 5 reversed

2
Cardinals in the Forest
Small Star
Cut 7

3
Cardinals in the Forest
Moon
Cut 4

1
Cardinals in the Forest
Large Star
Cut 6

5
Cardinals in the Forest
Stem
Cut 4 and 4 reversed

Poinsettia

By Karen Schoepflin Hagen

Poinsettia by Karen Schoepflin Hagen, 1989, Genesee, Idaho, 36" x 36" (irregular).

KAREN SCHOEPFLIN HAGEN

KAREN SCHOEPFLIN HAGEN DISCOV-ERED QUILTING IN 1975. ALTHOUGH HER FIRST QUILTS WERE MADE USING TRADI-TIONAL PATTERNS, SHE SOON BEGAN CREATING HER OWN DESIGNS. THROUGH-OUT THE SUMMER MONTHS, KAREN GOES TOURING WITH HER QUILTS, TAKING HER TRAVELING EXHIBIT TO AS MANY CITIES AS POSSIBLE EACH YEAR. SHE HOPES TO GIVE TO OTHERS SOME OF THE JOY SHE FINDS IN HER QUILTMAKING BY SHARING HER COM-PLETED QUILTS IN THIS WAY. SHE KEEPS HER QUILTS TOGETHER AS A "FAMILY" AND DREAMS OF SOMEDAY HOUSING HER QUILTMAKING LEGACY IN HER OWN QUILT MUSEUM.

KAREN WORKS FOR THE SCHOOL DISTRICT AS AN AIDE FOR A DISABLED CHILD. TRAINED AS A MUSICIAN, SHE TEACHES FLUTE AND PIANO AFTER SCHOOL HOURS. SHE STEALS SLEEP TIME TO MAKE QUILTS AFTER HER FAMILY HAS RETIRED FOR THE NIGHT.

KAREN DESIGNED THIS QUILT IN RE-SPONSE TO A CHALLENGE PROJECT WITH THE PALOUSE PATCHERS QUILT GUILD. THE LARGER-THAN-LIFE APPLIQUÉ FLOWER WAS ONE OF THREE WALL QUILTS SHE MADE FROM THE ALLOTTED FABRICS. TO COM-PLETE THE QUILT, SHE ADDED SEVERAL FABRICS TO THOSE IN THE CHALLENGE PACKET. IF YOU WOULD PREFER TO WORK WITH MORE THAN TWO RED FABRICS, SHE SUGGESTS USING A RED SOLID FOR ALL PIECES LABELED "A" AND ASSORTED RED PRINTS OR PLAIDS FOR ALL PIECES LABELED "B."

THIS QUILT WOULD BE BEAUTIFUL AS A TABLE TOPPER ON A RED TABLECLOTH OR AS A WALL HANGING.

Quilt Plan

Quilt Size: 36" x 36" (irregular)

Materials: 44"-wide fabric

1 yd. red solid for piece A

1 yd. red print or plaid, or assorted red prints and plaids, for piece B

1/2 yd. deep green print for piece C

6" x 6" piece of tan/cream print for flower center

7" x 10" rectangle of light green print for center underlay

40" x 40" piece of fabric for backing

40" x 40" piece of thin, compact batting

Large sheets of white tissue paper

Cutting

*Use the pattern on the pullout pattern
insert at the back of the book.*

1. Trace the pattern onto white tissue paper. Make a second tracing to cut apart into individual pattern pieces for color placement.

2. Referring to the color photo for placement, position the pattern pieces on the fabric so that the grain line runs from point to point on all leaves and petals. Cut out all fabric pieces, allowing seam allowances all around to turn under for appliqué. (See "Making Templates" on page 8 and "Marking and Cutting Fabric" on page 9.)

Assembling the Quilt Top and Finishing

1. Place the full-size tracing on a tabletop or other flat surface. Pin the light green rectangle in the center of the pattern, inside the area indicated.

2. Position the leaves (piece C) on the tracing, then add petals (piece B), followed by petals (piece A). Pin the pieces together where they overlap, avoiding pinning into the paper pattern.

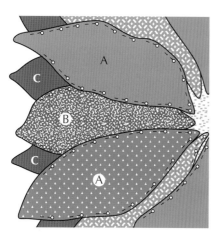

3. Remove the pin in the light green area and remove the paper pattern. To avoid working with so many pins, baste the layers together about ½" from the raw edges and then remove the pins. It will be easier—and safer—to handle the assemblage without the pins.

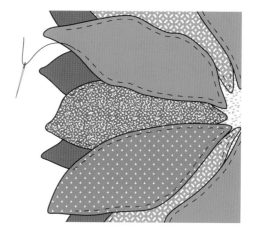

4. To ensure smooth, even results, work on a flat surface, such as a large breadboard or tabletop. Following the directions for "Needle-Turn Appliqué" on page 10, turn under the edges and stitch. Because this is a free-form design, don't worry about a little variance in the amount of fabric you turn under, but be sure there is sufficient overlap to adequately anchor the pieces together. Leave the last ¼" of all pieces unstitched to avoid clipping later. Do not turn under the outer edges of the petals. They will be caught in the seam that holds the backing in place.

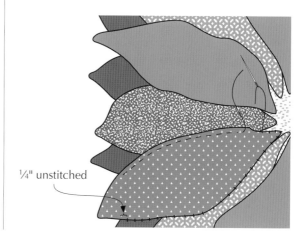

¼" unstitched

Finishing

1. Place the completed quilt top on top of the batting square and use safety pins to anchor the two layers together, keeping the pins away from the outer edges. Trim the batting even with the quilt top.

2. With right sides together, arrange the quilt top (with batting attached) into position over the backing. Trim the backing so that the edges of the backing, batting, and quilt top are all even. Use straight pins to secure the quilt layers around the outer edge.

3. Machine stitch ¼" from the raw edges, leaving an opening as marked on the pattern in order to turn the quilt right side out.

4. Clip the inner corners and trim the excess fabric from the points.

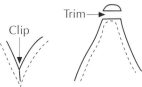

Clip

Trim→

5. Turn the quilt right side out. Using pointed scissors, gently push the points out from the inside. Press, making sure that the edge of the backing is not exposed along the outer edges.

6. Turn under the opening edges of the top and backing and slipstitch closed.

7. Baste or "safety-pin baste" through all layers to keep them from shifting while you quilt.

8. Quilt in-the-ditch around the outer edges of each petal and along the vein lines as marked on the pattern. (See page 16.)

9. From the cream/tan print, cut 11 or 12 circles, each about 1³/₈" in diameter. Do a gathering stitch ³/₁₆" from the raw edge of each circle. Draw up the stitches and tuck a bit of polyester fiberfill or a piece of batting inside. Tuck the raw edges inside the circle.

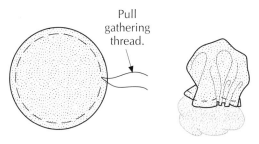

Pull gathering thread.

Place batting inside.

10. Arrange the circles in the flower center and appliqué in place, tucking in as needed to form a smooth, round puff.

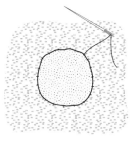

Appliqué in place.

11. Sign your quilt. (See page 18.)

Christmas Rose Trellis

By Lorre Weidlich

Christmas Rose Trellis by Lorre Weidlich, 1993, Austin, Texas, 29" x 29".

LORRE WEIDLICH

LORRE WEIDLICH BEGAN HER FIRST QUILT IN 1972. SHE FINISHED IT TWENTY YEARS LATER. DURING THOSE TWENTY YEARS, SHE BEGAN AND COMPLETED A NUMBER OF OTHER QUILTS, AS WELL AS BECOMING A QUILT TEACHER, DESIGNER, LECTURER, AND JUDGE. SHE ALSO COMPLETED A PH.D. IN FOLKLORE WITH A DISSERTATION DEVOTED TO THE CURRENT QUILT REVIVAL, SO SCHOLAR IS ANOTHER ROLE SHE PLAYS IN THE QUILT WORLD. HER ARTICLES HAVE BEEN PUBLISHED IN SEVERAL QUILTING PERIODICALS, AND HER QUILTS AND WEARABLE ART HAVE RECEIVED LOCAL AND NATIONAL RECOGNITION. SHE BALANCES HER AVAILABLE TIME BETWEEN MAKING QUILTS AND RESEARCHING AND WRITING ABOUT QUILTING.

"CHRISTMAS ROSE TRELLIS" BEGAN AS A SIMPLE PIECED BACKDROP TO USE BEHIND CHRISTMAS DECORATIONS. LORRE ADAPTED AND ENLARGED FOUR TRADITIONAL JACOB'S LADDER BLOCKS TO MAKE A WALL QUILT, BUT AFTER PIECING IT, SHE FOUND THAT THE SOLID GREEN CENTER AND CORNERS WERE TOO EMPTY. FILLING THEM WITH APPLIQUÉ WAS THE PERFECT ANSWER. THEN THE REST OF THE TOP, INCLUDING THE BORDERS, BEGGED FOR APPLIQUÉ AS WELL. LORRE'S LOVELY FLOWERS AND VINES CLEVERLY DISGUISE THE WELL-LOVED BLOCK! EVENTUALLY, LORRE FINISHED THE QUILT, ONLY NINE YEARS AFTER SHE STARTED IT! THE ROSE TRELLIS CLASS HAS BEEN ONE OF LORRE'S MOST POPULAR QUILT WORKSHOPS.

Quilt Plan

Quilt Size: 29" x 29"

Materials: 44"-wide fabric

¼ yd. white tone-on-tone print for appliquéd flowers and buds

⅜ yd. light green solid for vines, leaves, buds, and flower center

⅞ yd. medium green solid for borders, corners, center, and leaves, buds, and vines

¼ yd. dark green solid for four-patch units

¼ yd. red-and-green print for four-patch units

¼ yd. green print for half-square triangles

⅞ yd. red print for binding, inner borders, half-square triangles, and center flower

⅞ yd. for backing

32" x 32" piece of batting

Thread for appliqué to match appliqué fabrics

Cutting

Use the appliqué templates on page 67. Refer to "Basic Appliqué" on pages 8–11 for information on how to make templates and cut them from your fabric.

From the white tone-on-tone print, cut:
    1 of Template 1 (center flower);
    12 of Template 5 (flowers on vines);
    12 of Template 7 (buds).

From the light green solid, cut:
    8 bias strips, each $3/4$" x 15", for border vines;
    48 of Template 4 (leaves);
    4 of Template 6 (base for bud);
    1 of Template 3 (center flower).

From the medium green solid, cut:
    4 middle border strips, each $2^1/2$" x 30",
        cutting along the fabric length;
    1 square, $8^1/2$" x $8^1/2$", for center;
    4 squares, each $4^1/2$" x $4^1/2$", for corners;
    8 bias strips, each $3/4$" x 11", for vines;
    24 of Template 4 (leaves);
    8 of Template 6 (base for bud).

From the dark green solid, cut:
    2 strips, each $2^1/2$" x 42", for four-patch units.

From the red-and-green print, cut:
    2 strips, each $2^1/2$" x 42", for four-patch units.

From the green print, cut:
    8 squares, each $4^7/8$" x $4^7/8$", for bias squares.

From the red print, cut:
    4 binding strips, each $2^1/2$" wide and the fabric length;
    8 inner and outer border strips, each $3/4$" x 30", cutting along the fabric length;
    8 squares, each $4^7/8$" x $4^7/8$", for bias squares;
    1 of Template 2 (center flower).

Piecing the Corner and Side Units

All seam allowances are $1/4$" wide.

1. Using the $4^7/8$" x $4^7/8$" squares of the red print and the green print, follow the instructions for cut-and-pieced squares on page 8. You should have a total of 16 bias squares. Press the seams toward the red print in 8 of the units and toward the green print in the remaining 8 units.

Make 16

2. With right sides together, sew each $2^1/2$" x 42" dark green strip to a $2^1/2$" x 42" red-and-green print strip. Press the seam toward the dark green strip in each strip-pieced unit. Crosscut a total of 24 segments, each $2^1/2$"-wide.

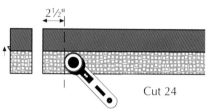

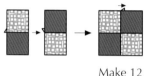

Cut 24

3. Assemble 12 four-patch units as shown and press the seam to one side in each unit.

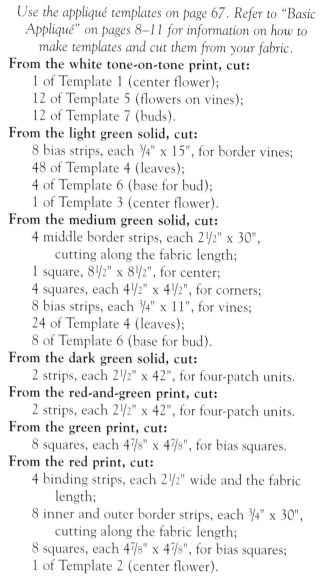

Make 12

4. To assemble each of the 4 corner units, arrange 1 four-patch unit, 2 bias squares, and one $4^1/2$" x $4^1/2$" medium green square as shown. Sew the units together in horizontal rows and press the seams in opposite directions as shown. Sew the rows together to complete each unit; press.

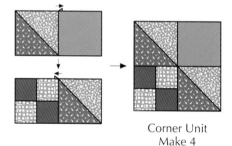

Corner Unit
Make 4

5. To assemble each of the 4 side units, arrange 2 four-patch units and 2 bias squares as shown, paying careful attention to color placement. Sew the units together in horizontal rows and press the seams in opposite directions as shown. Sew the rows together to complete each unit; press.

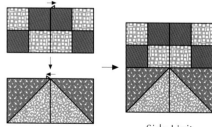

Side Unit
Make 4

Assembling the Quilt Top

1. Arrange the 4 corner units, the 4 side units, and the 8¹/₂" medium green square in 3 rows as shown. Sew the units together in horizontal rows, pressing the seams in opposite directions from row to row.

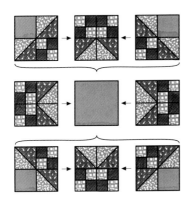

2. Sew the rows together to complete the pieced quilt top; press.

3. Sew a narrow red print border strip to the sides of each of the 4 medium green middle border strips. Press the seams toward the green strip in each border unit.

Make 4

4. Attach the borders to each side of the quilt top, following the directions for "Borders with Mitered Corners" on page 14. Before stitching the mitered corner, make sure that the border seam lines match perfectly where they meet.

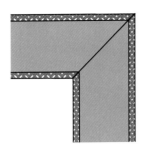

Appliquéing the Flowers and Vines

Preventing Color Show-Through on Light Appliqués

Before you begin, place a scrap of the white tone-on-tone fabric on top of the various fabrics in the quilt top to make sure that the colors and the turned edges of the appliqué will not show through the white fabric. If they do, cut a lining layer for each white appliqué from a lightweight white fabric, such as batiste, but do not include seam allowances in the lining pieces. Baste the lining to the wrong side of each appliqué piece and do not remove this basting until after the quilt has been quilted. The quilting stitches will hold the lining in place.

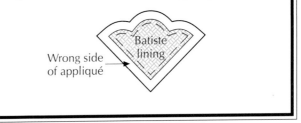

Wrong side of appliqué — Batiste lining

1. Mark the center of the green square in the quilt top by folding the square on each diagonal and finger-pressing. Then fold the square in half horizontally and vertically. Use these lines to position the white central flower (Template 1). Pin in place and appliqué. Next add the red layer of the flower (Template 2) and the green center (Template 3). When you appliqué these top two layers, take care to stitch only through the layer just below, not all the way down to the green layer. This will allow you to easily cut out the background layers before layering the quilt top with batting and backing in preparation for quilting. Position the leaves on the crease lines, pin in place, and appliqué.

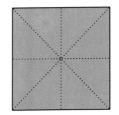

Crease center square.   Use fold lines for positioning.

2. Make the light green and medium green vines using the bias strips you cut, referring to "Making Bias Stems" on page 11.

3. Position the vines, referring to the quilt photo and the quilt plan. Baste in place, then appliqué. (Basting is recommended because it is difficult to make bias strips follow a smooth curve if you use pins to hold them in place.)

4. To position leaves, buds, and flowers, refer to the quilt photo and quilt plan. To assist you in precise positioning of the flowers in the corners, crease (or mark) a diagonal line through each medium green square. Line up the white flower so that its center and its point and both points of the leaf below it are on the diagonal crease.

Line up corner flower
with diagonal crease.

To position the white flowers around the center square, use the seam line between the two green print triangles as a guide. Line up the flowers so that their centers and points fall on the seam lines. Pin in place and appliqué.

5. Position both the white and green pieces of each bud before appliquéing them in place to ensure that the green piece covers the raw edges of both the white bud and the bias strip vine. Pin. Appliqué the white piece first, then the green. The green piece, with its two inside points, is the most difficult piece to appliqué. Simplify it, if necessary, by eliminating the middle point.

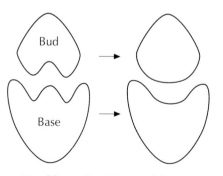

Bud

Base

Simplify appliqué shapes if desired.

Finishing

1. Carefully cut out the back layers behind the center flower, the white flowers, and the buds. It is not necessary to cut out the background behind the leaves.

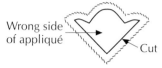

Wrong side
of appliqué

Cut

2. Mark the quilting design onto the quilt top, following the illustration below.

Quilting Suggestion

3. Layer the quilt top with batting and backing; baste.

4. Quilt on the marked lines. In addition, quilt around each appliqué. (See page 16.)

5. Bind the edges with 2½"-wide red print strips. (See pages 17–18.)

6. Sign your quilt. (See page 18.)

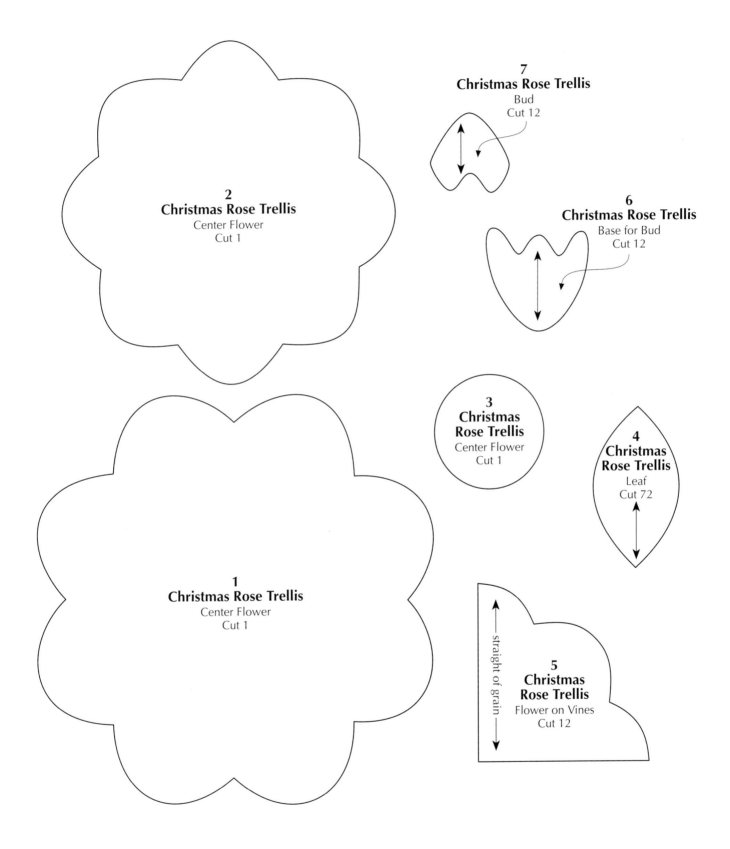

7
Christmas Rose Trellis
Bud
Cut 12

6
Christmas Rose Trellis
Base for Bud
Cut 12

2
Christmas Rose Trellis
Center Flower
Cut 1

3
Christmas
Rose Trellis
Center Flower
Cut 1

4
Christmas
Rose Trellis
Leaf
Cut 72

1
Christmas Rose Trellis
Center Flower
Cut 1

straight of grain

5
Christmas
Rose Trellis
Flower on Vines
Cut 12

Celestial Selection

By Melody Crust

Celestial Selection by Melody Crust, 1993,
Kent, Washington, 35^1/$_2$" x 35^1/$_2$".

Celestial Selection (variation)

MELODY CRUST

MELODY IS A FIRST-GENERATION QUILTER WHOSE LOVE OF FABRIC AND QUILTMAKING HAS LED HER TO DESIGN, TEACH, LECTURE, AND PUBLISH. HER WORK IS FOUND IN PRIVATE COLLECTIONS AND GALLERIES AND HAS BEEN PUBLISHED IN *QUILTER'S NEWSLETTER MAGAZINE*. MANY OF HER ORIGINAL QUILTS HAVE WON AWARDS AT REGIONAL AND NATIONAL QUILT SHOWS, INCLUDING A HOFFMAN CHALLENGE COMPETITION. SHE HAS ALSO DESIGNED AND SELF-PUBLISHED A LINE OF QUILT-LABEL PATTERNS TO ENCOURAGE QUILTERS TO PERMANENTLY IDENTIFY THEIR QUILTS.

AN ACTIVE MEMBER OF THREE QUILT GUILDS, MELODY CO-FOUNDED AND IS VICE PRESIDENT OF THE ASSOCIATION OF PACIFIC NORTHWEST QUILTERS. IN 1994, APNQ PRODUCED THE FIRST JUDGED AND JURIED QUILT EXHIBITION IN THE NORTHWEST.

CHRISTMAS, WITH ITS SUMPTUOUS COLORS AND FESTIVE MOOD, IS MELODY'S FAVORITE TIME OF YEAR. IN "CELESTIAL SELECTION," SHE EXPERIMENTED WITH SELECTIVE CUTTING. BY ISOLATING SPECIFIC AREAS IN A RICHLY PATTERNED FLORAL STRIPE, SHE CREATED FOUR VERY DIFFERENT, DAZZLING STARS. THE EFFECT? MAGIC!

Quilt Plan

Quilt Size: 35½" x 35½"*
Block Size: 12" x 12"

Materials: 44"-wide fabric

2½ yds. floral stripe for selectively cut stars, sashing, and outer border**

¾ yd. dark print for background and binding

¼ yd. gold lamé for inner border

1½ yds. for backing and hanging sleeve

39" x 39" piece of batting

* Varies, depending on the border width you choose.

** The patterned stripe shown has 9 repeats across the width. If your fabric has fewer repeats, you will need more yardage.

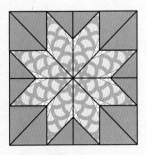

12" Block

Cutting

Use the template on page 71.

Apply ¼" quilter's masking tape to the template perimeter to "preview" a finished piece. Once you select an area of the design and cut one piece, mark the template in pencil to guide you in cutting identical pieces.

From the lengthwise grain of the floral stripe, cut:

4 strips, for outer border. Strip width is equal to area you want to feature, plus ½" for seam allowances; 4½" to 6½" is a typical cut width. Strip length is estimated finished quilt size (including borders), plus 3". (See page 14.)

2 strips, each 2½" x 12½", for sashing;

1 strip, 2½" x 26½", for sashing;

8 of Template A from each of 4 different areas for a total of 32 for Star blocks.

From the dark print for background, cut:

2 strips, each 3⅜" x 42", for star background; crosscut strips into 16 squares, each 3⅜" x 3⅜", then cut squares once diagonally to yield 32 of piece B;

2 strips, each 4⅜" x 42", for star background; crosscut strips into 16 squares, each 4⅜" x 4⅜", then cut squares once diagonally to yield 32 of piece C.

From the gold lamé, cut:

4 strips, each 1" x 42", for inner border.

Piecing the Star Blocks

1. Sew piece A and piece B together as shown. Press the seam toward piece B and trim the "dog ears." Sew a matching piece C to piece AB as shown to make unit 1. Press the seam toward piece C and trim. Make a total of 4 units for each star.

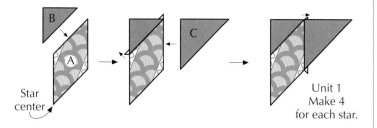

2. Sew a matching piece A and piece B together as shown. Press the seam toward piece A and trim. Sew a matching piece C to piece AB as shown to make unit 2. Press the seam toward piece AB and trim. Make a total of 4 units for each star.

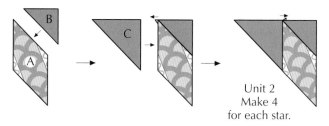

Unit 2
Make 4
for each star.

3. Join a matching unit 1 and unit 2, making sure to match opposing seams, to make 1 quarter-section. Make a total of 4 quarter-sections for each star. Press the seams in the same direction.

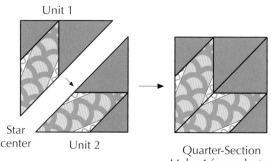

Quarter-Section
Make 4 for each star.

4. Arrange 4 matching quarter-sections as shown. Sew the top quarter-sections together; press the seam to the left. Sew the bottom quarter-sections together; press the seam to the right. Join the 2 units to complete 1 Star block. Press the seam down. Using the remaining background pieces and star pieces cut from other sections of the floral stripe, make a total of 4 Star blocks.

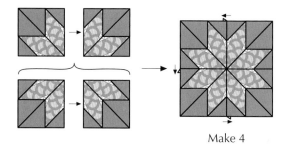

Make 4

Assembling the Quilt Top and Finishing

1. Arrange the 4 Star blocks and sashing strips as shown. Sew the blocks and short sashing strips in 2 vertical rows. Press the seams toward the sashing strips. Join the rows and the long sashing strip, making sure the Star blocks and short sashing strips align horizontally. Press the seams toward the sashing strip.

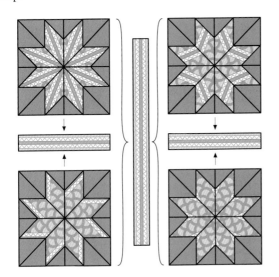

2. Attach the border, following the directions for "Borders with Mitered Corners" on page 14. You may find it easier to match the designs in the borders if you hand stitch the mitered corners from the top.
3. Mark the quilt top as desired.
4. Layer the quilt top with batting and backing; baste.
5. Quilt on the marked lines. (See page 16.)
6. Bind the edges with 2½"-wide straight-grain strips of dark print. (See pages 17–18.)
7. Sign your quilt. (See page 18.)

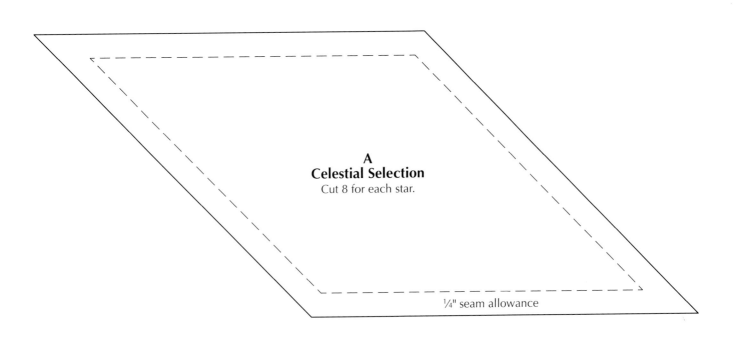

A
Celestial Selection
Cut 8 for each star.

¼" seam allowance

A Woodland Family Christmas

By Leslie Beck

A Woodland Family Christmas by Leslie Beck, 1994, Kennewick, Washington, 28" x 34½".

LESLIE BECK

LESLIE HAS LED A VARIED AND EXCITING LIFE AS AN ARTIST. SHE COMES FROM A CREATIVE FAMILY: HER GRANDFATHER WAS A CABINETMAKER IN NORWAY, AND HER MOTHER CRAFTED AND SOLD WAXED FLOWERS. LESLIE SAYS SHE AND HER BROTHERS "GREW UP WITH PENCILS, PAPER, CRAYONS, PASTE, AND A HEALTHY IMAGINATION. AS A CHILD, I LOVED COLLAGE. I STILL DO. AND I CALL IT QUILTING."

LESLIE FOUNDED HER OWN WEAVING COMPANY, FIBER MOSAICS, AND BEGAN DESIGNING AND MARKETING SANTAS AND DOLLS, A PURSUIT THAT HAS DEVELOPED INTO A FULL-TIME BUSINESS, WITH MORE THAN NINETY ORIGINAL PATTERNS. FOR FIVE YEARS, SHE DESIGNED QUILTING AND FLANNEL FABRICS FOR FABRIC SALES COMPANY IN SEATTLE. CURRENTLY, SHE DESIGNS PRINTS FOR V.I.P. FABRICS. IN ADDITION TO ALL OF THESE CREATIVE ENDEAVORS, LESLIE HAS WRITTEN A NUMBER OF BOOKS.

MANY OF LESLIE'S DESIGNS ARE WALL HANGINGS THAT FEATURE NO-SEW APPLIQUÉ USING PAPER-BACKED FUSIBLE WEB, A TECHNIQUE THAT ALLOWS HER TO CREATE INTRICATE-LOOKING IMAGES QUICKLY. SHE OFTEN STRIP-PIECES THE BORDERS, ANOTHER FAST-AND-EASY METHOD FOR QUILTERS WHO HAVE THE DESIRE—BUT NOT THE TIME—TO MAKE COMPLEX PROJECTS.

LESLIE FINDS MAGIC IN THE INNOCENCE OF CHILDREN AND SMALL ANIMALS. "A WOODLAND FAMILY CHRISTMAS" WAS INSPIRED BY MEMORIES OF THE WONDERFUL CHRISTMAS STORIES HER CHILDREN ENJOYED, STORIES THAT NOW DELIGHT HER GRANDSON GABE. "I LIKE TO THINK THAT SANTA BRINGS WARMTH AND CARING TO ALL OF GOD'S CREATURES AT CHRISTMASTIME."

Quilt Plan

Quilt Size: 28" x 34½"

Materials: 44"-wide fabric

¾ yd. blue fabric for background, pieced background, and pieced border

⅓ yd. holiday print for pieced background and pieced border

¼ yd. each gold, green, and red prints for pieced background and pieced border. For a scrappy look, use a variety of prints, making sure you have a total of ¼ yd. or more of each color.

⅛ yd. brown print for pieced border

¼ yd. black print for sashing

¼ yd. green print for tree

¼ yd. red print for Santa suit

¼ yd. white print for Santa beard, snowman, and snow. For visual interest, use a variety of white prints, making sure you have a total of ¼ yd. or more.

(continued on page 74)

Materials: (continued from page 73)

⅛ yd. each of assorted prints or scraps for remaining appliqué pieces

1 yd. paper-backed fusible web, such as HeatnBond®

½ yd. lightweight fusible woven interfacing

Fine-line black permanent fabric marker

1 yd. for backing

32" x 38" piece of batting

⅓ yd. black solid for binding

Craft needle

Black and gold embroidery floss

Buttons: 17 white, ½" to 1" in diameter; 7 red, ⅜" in diameter; 5 black, ¼" in diameter; and 2 brown, ½" in diameter

Fabric glue

Cotton-tipped swab and blush for Santa and mice cheeks

Cutting			
Color	**No. Pieces**	**Dimensions**	**Section**
Background			
Blue	1	6¾" x 12"	Birdhouse (A)
	1	6" x 8"	Mittens (B)
	1	7" x 11"	Snowman (C)
	1	10" x 12"	Santa (D)
	1	12" X 17"	Trees (E)

Cutting continued		
Color	**No. Pieces**	**Dimensions**
Pieced background*		
Blue	1	1¾" x 42"
H'day print	1	2" x 42"
Gold	1	1¼" x 42"
Green	1	1½" x 42"
Red	1	1¼" x 42"
Pieced border*		
Blue	1	1¼" x 42"
	1	2" x 42"
H'day print	2	1¾" x 42"
	1	2½" x 42"
	1	3" x 42"
Gold	1	1½" x 42"
	1	2¼" x 42"
Green	1	1¼" x 42"
	1	2" x 42"
	1	2¾" x 42"
Red	1	1¼" x 42"
	1	1½" x 42"
	1	1¾" x 42"
Brown	1	1¾" x 42"

*Keep the strips for the pieced background and pieced border in separate groups.

Sashing—Black print			
First Cut		**Second Cut**	
No. Strips	**Strip Width**	**No. Pieces**	**Dimensions**
5	1¼"	2	1¼" x 12"
		2	1¼" x 23¾"
		2	1¼" x 29¼"
		1	1¼" x 8"
		1	1¼" x 10"
		1	1¼" x 17"
		1	1¼" x 22¼"

Piecing the Quilt Top

1. Cut the strips for the pieced background in half to yield strips approximately 21" long. With right sides together and varying the colors, join the strips to make 1 pieced unit, approximately 11" x 21". Change directions after sewing each strip and press the seams in the same direction.

2. Refer to the diagram below to cut the following pieces for the pieced background: 5¾" x 8", 1½" x 7", 1½" x 10", and 3¾" x 10".

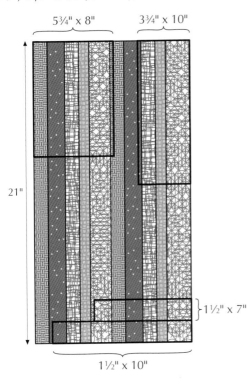

3. Join Mittens and Mice section B, the 8" sashing strip, and the 5¾" x 8" pieced background unit. Press the seams (and all following sashing seams) toward the sashing strip. Join Snowman section C and the 1½" x 7" pieced background unit. Join sections A, B, and C, with two 12" sashing strips in between.

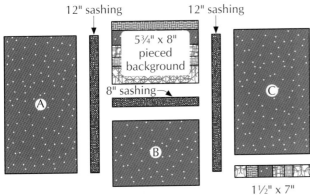

4. Join Santa section D, the 1½" x 10" pieced background unit, the 10" sashing strip, and the 3¾" x 10" pieced background unit. Join section D and Trees section E, with the 17" sashing strip in between.

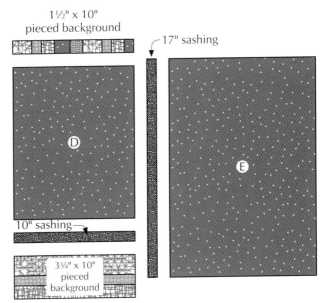

5. Join the upper and lower sections of the quilt top, with the 22¼" sashing strip in between.

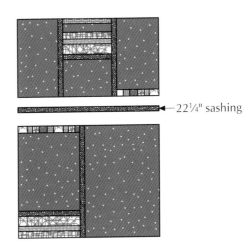

6. Sew the 29¼" sashing strips to the right and left edges of the quilt top. Then sew the 23¾" sashing strips to the top and bottom edges of the quilt top.

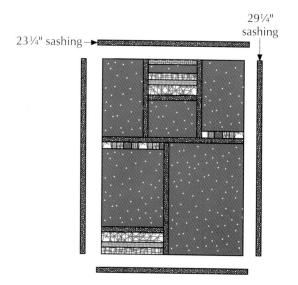

23¾" sashing →

29¼" sashing

7. Cut the strips for the pieced border in half to yield strips approximately 21" long. With right sides together and varying the colors, join the strips to make 1 pieced unit, approximately 21" x 31½". Change directions after sewing each strip and press the seams in the same direction.

8. Cut the following pieces for the pieced border: 2 pieces, each 2½" x 30¾", for the side borders, and 2 pieces, each 2½" x 27¾", for the top and bottom borders.

9. Sew the 30¾" pieced border strips to the sides of the quilt top. Then sew the 27¾" pieced border strips to the top and bottom edges of the quilt top.

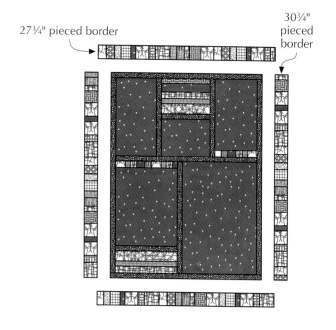

27¾" pieced border

30¾" pieced border

Appliquéing the Quilt Top

Use the patterns on pages 78–85.

For best results when fusing the pieces, follow the manufacturer's instructions carefully. Be sure to use the recommended heat settings; an iron that's too hot will cause the adhesive to come through the fabrics, and the pieces won't stick. Back the off-white fabrics and fabric for Santa's face with fusible interfacing to prevent the dark fabrics from showing through.

1. Trace each appliqué piece on the paper side of the fusible web, leaving ½" between pieces. (The pieces as they are drawn are "flopped"; when you fuse them to the background, they will appear as they do in the photo.) Cut out the pieces, leaving a ¼" allowance.

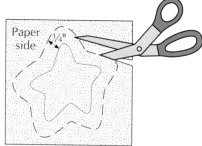

Paper side

¼"

2. Place the fabric, wrong side up, on your ironing surface. Lay the fusible web, paper side up, on the fabric. Fuse. After the fabric has cooled, cut out the appliqué on the pencil line. Repeat for the other pieces.

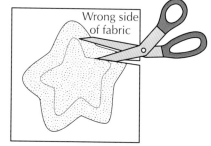

Wrong side of fabric

3. Leave the paper backing on the larger pieces. Remove the paper backing on the small pieces and fuse them to the larger ones, such as the toes and heels to the stockings. Don't fuse the noses to the mice, or the mittens to the background yet.

4. Fuse the pieces to the background. If any of the pieces lift, turn the quilt over and fuse from the back, or place a book on top of the fused area and apply pressure until the fabrics cool.

Finishing

1. Using the permanent marker, draw quilting "stitches" 1/16" to 1/8" long on the edges of the light appliqué pieces. Outline the pieces, drawing as close to the edges as possible.
2. Mark the quilt top as desired.
3. Layer the quilt top with batting and backing; baste.
4. Quilt on the marked lines. (See page 16.)
5. Bind the edges with 2½"-wide black strips. (See pages 17–18.)
6. Thread a craft needle with three strands of black embroidery floss; don't knot the end. Position a white button on the pieced background or border and sew through one button hole to the back of the quilt, leaving a 2" tail. Sew through the second button hole to the top of the quilt.

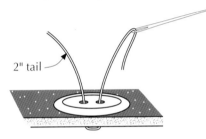

2" tail

Tie the floss tails together on top of the button. Place a dot of fabric glue on the knot and trim the tails to ¼". Sew the remaining white buttons randomly to the quilt top.

7. For the snowman, sew ¼" black buttons for the eyes and down the front. Sew a ½" red button to the scarf at the shoulder.
8. For the tree, cut an 18" length of black floss. Sew a ½" black button to the top of tree, but don't cut the floss after tying the knot. Position a second ½" button about 2" from the first. Leaving 2" of floss free, sew the second button to the tree. Continuing in the same manner, sew 4 more ½" black buttons down the tree.

9. For the mittens and mice, cut two 10" pieces of gold floss. Holding the pieces together, tie an overhand knot about ½" from each end. Lay the floss on the background; position the mittens over the floss; fuse. Cut a 1" piece of black floss. Divide the floss into two 3-strand pieces and lay each piece on a mouse face; fuse each nose over the floss. Trim and spread the floss ends. Sew a ½" brown button over the gold floss at each knot.
10. Using the permanent marker and referring to the quilt plan, write the following: "Byrd" on the birdhouse sign; "Dear Crossing" on the fence signs; and "Byrd seed," "Mice treats," "Snowman candy," "Dear feed," "Dog bones," and "Cat" on Santa's list.
11. Draw the faces on Santa and the mice. Using a cotton-tipped swab, place a dot of blush on the cheeks.

12. Sign your quilt. (See page 18.)

A Woodland Family Christmas
Trace 1 of each piece unless otherwise indicated.

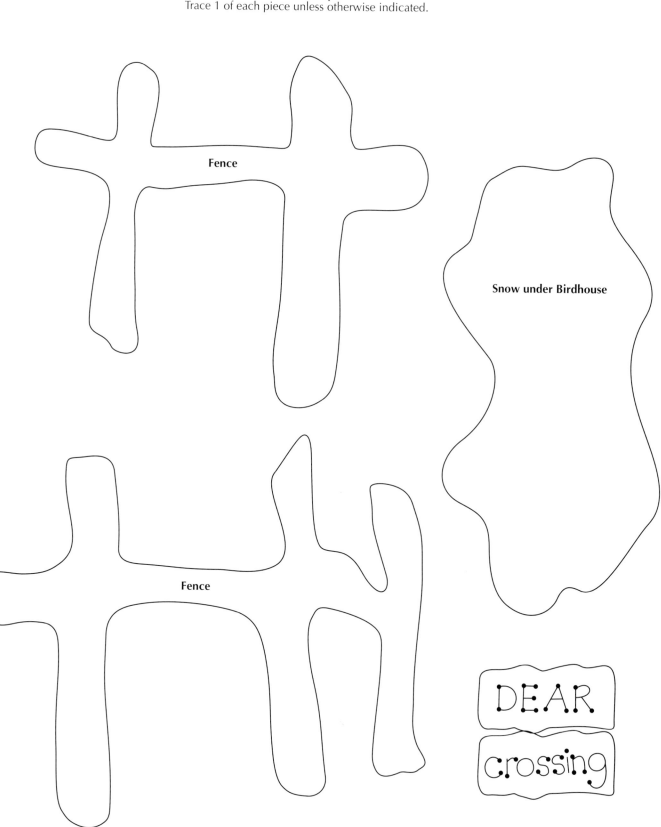

Fence

Snow under Birdhouse

Fence

DEAR
crossing

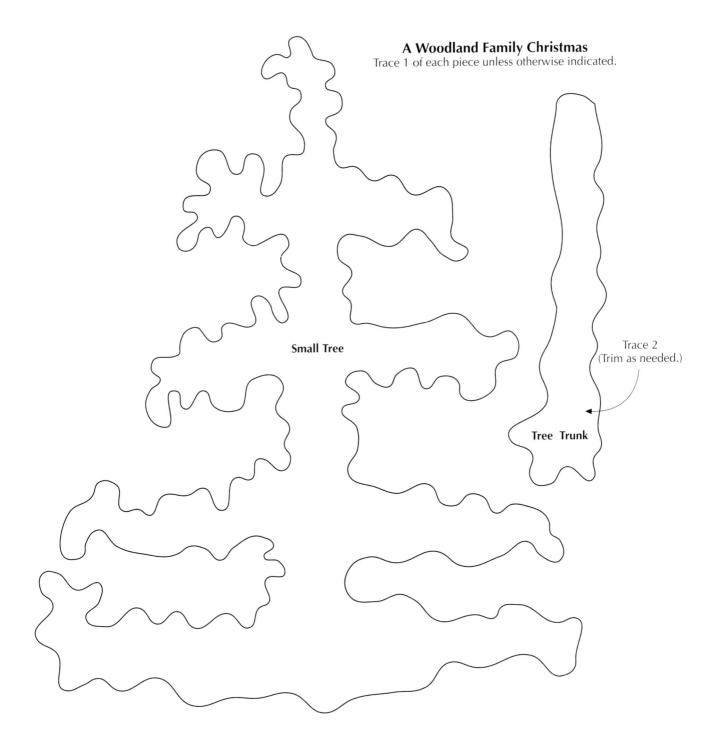

A Woodland Family Christmas
Trace 1 of each piece unless otherwise indicated.

Small Tree

Tree Trunk

Trace 2
(Trim as needed.)

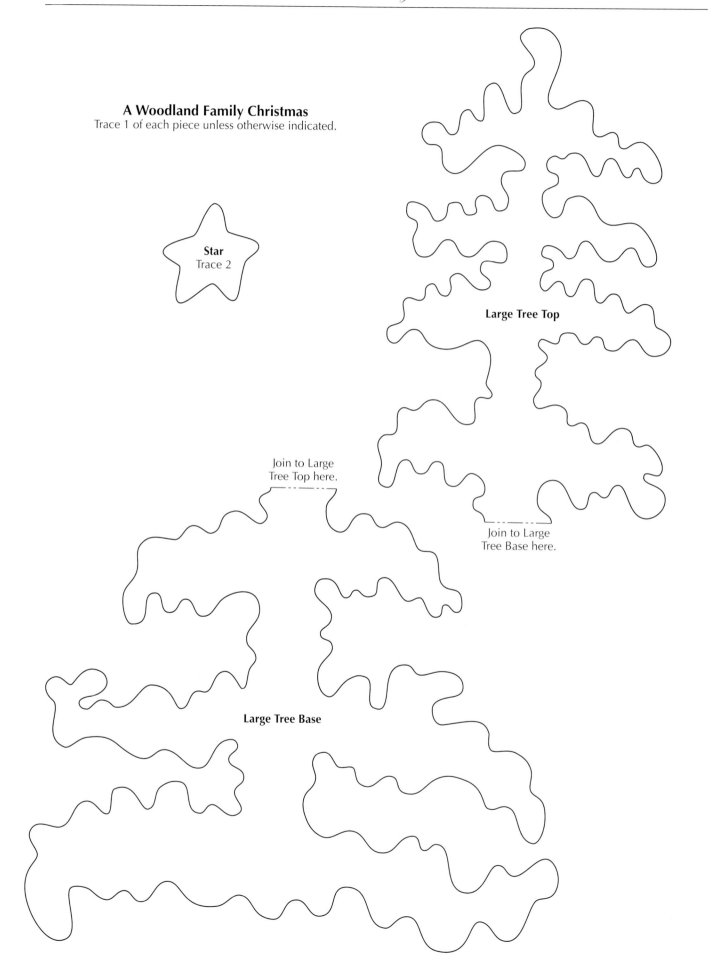

A Woodland Family Christmas
Trace 1 of each piece unless otherwise indicated.

Star
Trace 2

Large Tree Top

Join to Large
Tree Top here.

Join to Large
Tree Base here.

Large Tree Base

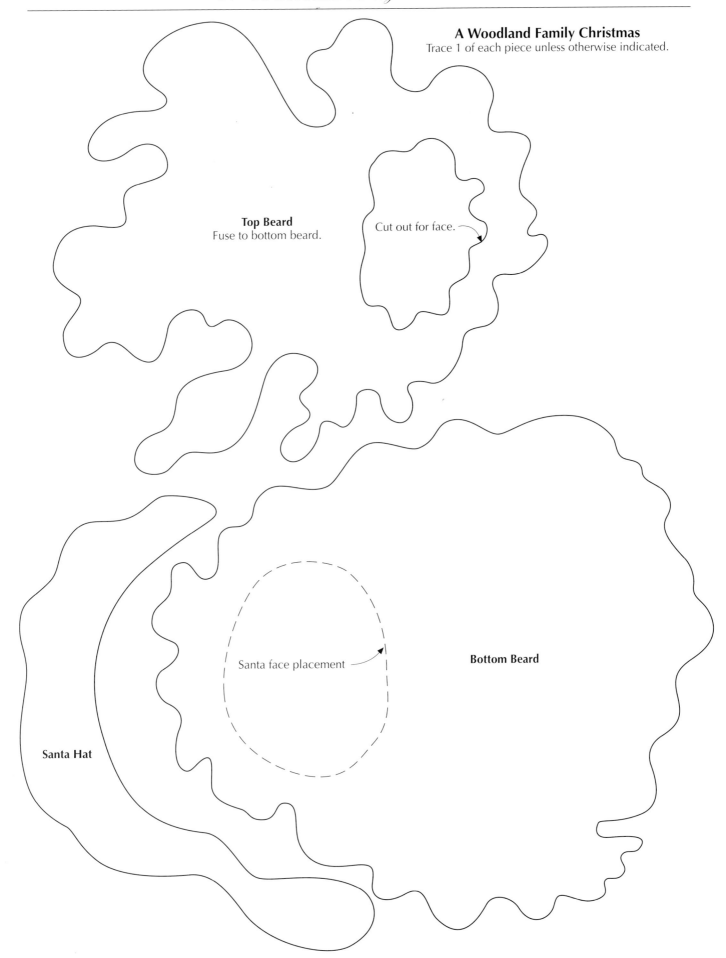

A Woodland Family Christmas
Trace 1 of each piece unless otherwise indicated.

Top Beard
Fuse to bottom beard.

Cut out for face.

Santa face placement

Bottom Beard

Santa Hat

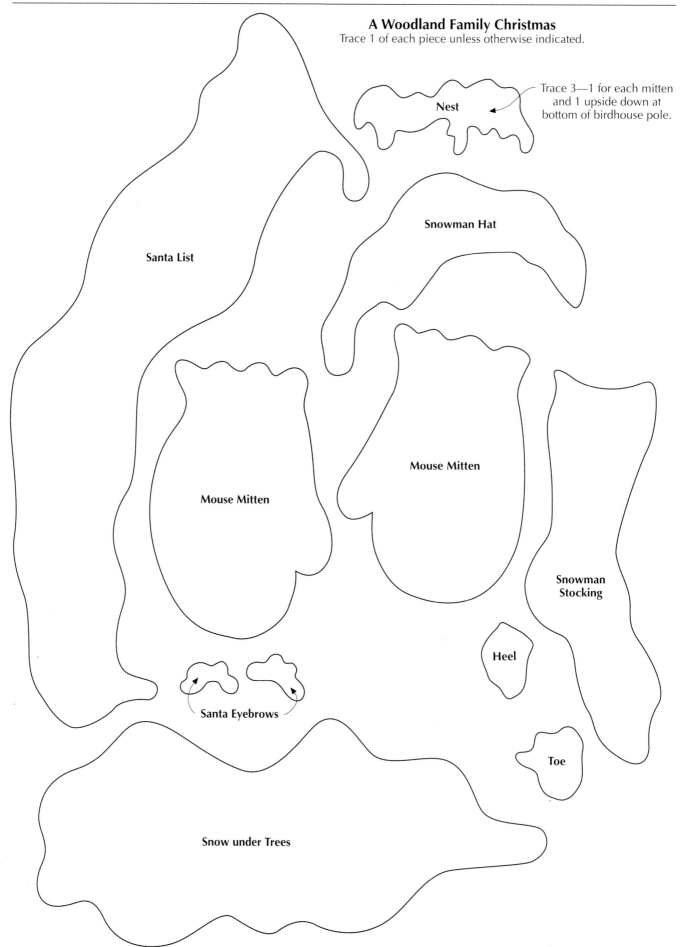

A Woodland Family Christmas
Trace 1 of each piece unless otherwise indicated.

Nest

Trace 3—1 for each mitten
and 1 upside down at
bottom of birdhouse pole.

Santa List

Snowman Hat

Mouse Mitten

Mouse Mitten

Snowman
Stocking

Heel

Santa Eyebrows

Toe

Snow under Trees

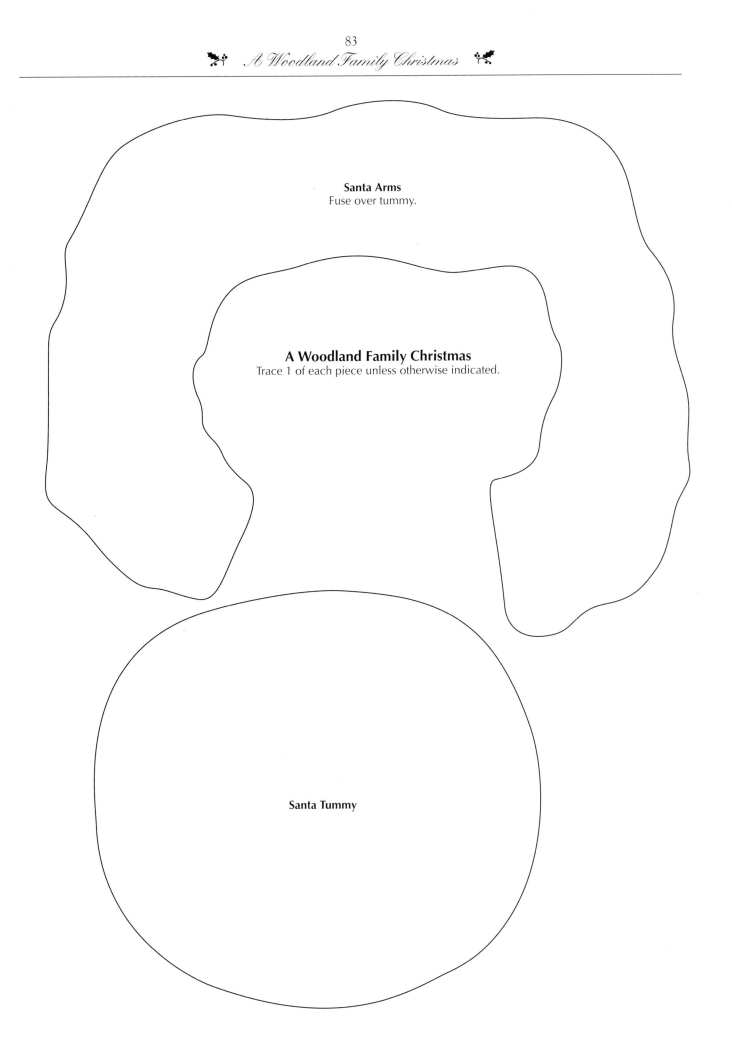

Santa Arms
Fuse over tummy.

A Woodland Family Christmas
Trace 1 of each piece unless otherwise indicated.

Santa Tummy

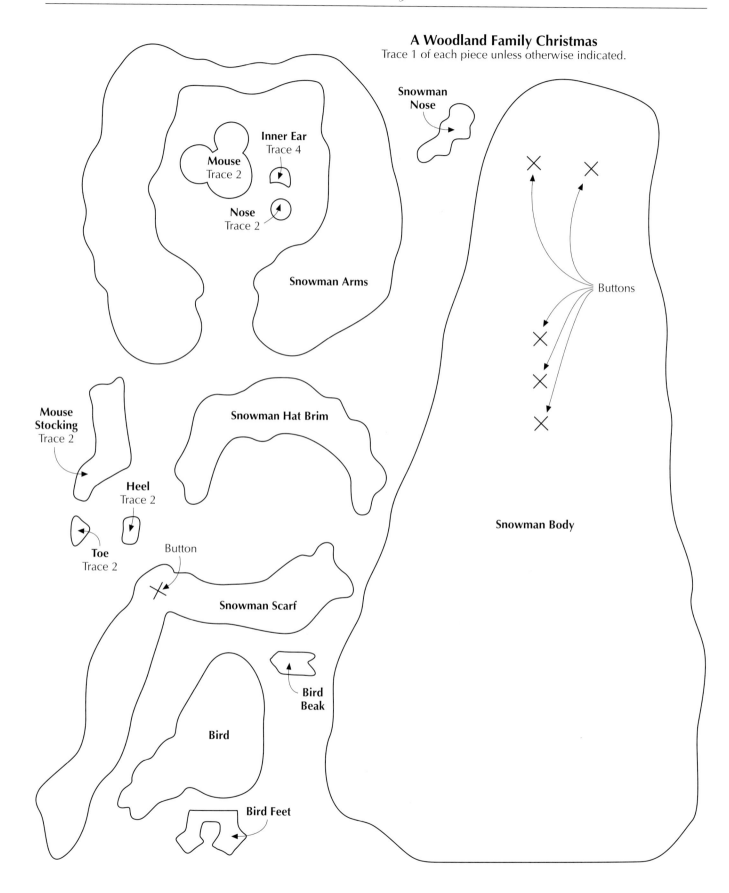

A Woodland Family Christmas
Trace 1 of each piece unless otherwise indicated.

Snowman
Nose

Mouse
Trace 2

Inner Ear
Trace 4

Nose
Trace 2

Snowman Arms

Buttons

**Mouse
Stocking**
Trace 2

Snowman Hat Brim

Heel
Trace 2

Toe
Trace 2

Button

Snowman Scarf

Snowman Body

**Bird
Beak**

Bird

Bird Feet

A Woodland Family Christmas

Trace 1 of each piece unless otherwise indicated.

Birdhouse Roof

Birdhouse Pole

Stocking
Trace 4

Heel
Trace 4

Birdhouse Sign

Toe
Trace 4

Birdhouse

Birdhouse
Hole

Santa "stash"

Santa Glove

Santa Cuff

Santa Face

Santa Glove

Santa Cuff

Cranberry Wreath

By Retta Warehime

Cranberry Wreath by Retta Warehime, 1994, Kennewick, Washington, 65" x 83".
Quilted by Vi McDonald, Spokane, Washington.

RETTA WAREHIME

RETTA HAS BEEN TEACHING PIECING FOR MORE THAN SIXTEEN YEARS AT QUILT SHOPS ALL OVER THE COUNTRY AND AT LOCAL COLLEGES. SHE DESIGNS AND MARKETS PATTERNS FOR HER COMPANY, SEW CHERISHED, WHICH OFFERS MORE THAN FIFTY-FIVE ORIGINAL DESIGNS. HER FIRST BOOK, *SEASONED WITH QUILTS*, IS A PART OF THE DESIGNER SERIES FROM THAT PATCHWORK PLACE.

IN ADDITION TO BEING AN AVID QUILTMAKER, RETTA IS A GARDENER, SKIER, MOTHER, AND FRIEND. SHE CLAIMS THAT SHE WILL EAT ANYTHING SHE DOESN'T HAVE TO COOK!

RETTA'S SPECIALTY IS FIGURING OUT HOW TO ELIMINATE TEMPLATES IN TRADITIONAL PATTERNS, AS WELL AS IN HER ORIGINAL DESIGNS. SHE DESIGNED HER ROTARY-CUT, NO-TEMPLATE "CRANBERRY WREATH" ESPECIALLY FOR THIS EDITION OF *QUILTED FOR CHRISTMAS*. RETTA SAW THE BLOCK IN AN OLD MAGAZINE BUT, AFTER LOOKING THROUGH MANY PATTERN BOOKS, COULD NOT DISCOVER ITS NAME. WITH THE HELP OF FRIENDS, SHE DECIDED TO CALL IT "CRANBERRY WREATH." SHE ORIGINALLY SET THE BLOCKS STRAIGHT, BUT LAURA REINSTATLER AT THAT PATCHWORK PLACE SUGGESTED A DIAGONAL SET, AND RETTA LIKED THE DESIGN EVEN MORE. "NEVER LIMIT YOURSELF TO ONE IDEA," SHE SAYS. "THERE MAY BE A BETTER DESIGN JUST WAITING—IT COULD BE YOUR 'CRANBERRY WREATH.'"

Quilt Plan

Quilt Size: 65" x 83"
Finished Block Size: 12" x 12"

Materials: 44"-wide fabric

3³⁄₄ yds. tan for background and border

⁵⁄₈ yd. medium dark red (Red 1) for blocks

⁵⁄₈ yd. dark red (Red 2) for blocks

1 yd. dark red (Red 3) for blocks

¹⁄₂ yd. light red (Red 4) for blocks

1⁷⁄₈ yds. dark red (Red 5) for blocks, sashing, inner border, and binding

¹⁄₂ yd. light red (Red 6) for blocks

¹⁄₈ yd. dark green for sashing squares

5 yds. for backing

68" x 86" piece of batting

12" Block

Cutting

Cut all strips across the fabric width (crosswise grain).

Fabric	No.Strips	Strip Width	No.Pieces	Dimensions
	First Cut		**Second Cut**	
Tan	3	$2^3/8"$	36	$2^3/8" \times 2^3/8"$
	7	$2"$	144	$2" \times 2"$
	7	$3^1/2"$	144	$2" \times 3^1/2"$
	3	$6^1/2"$	18	$6^1/2" \times 6^1/2"$
Red 1	4	$2"$	72	$2" \times 2"$
	2	$3^1/2"$	36	$2" \times 3^1/2"$
Red 2	4	$2"$	72	$2" \times 2"$
	2	$3^1/2"$	36	$2" \times 3^1/2"$
Red 3	12	$2"$	216	$2" \times 2"$
	3	$2^3/8"$	36	$2^3/8" \times 2^3/8"$
Red 4	4	$3^1/2"$	72	$2" \times 3^1/2"$
Red 5	4	$3^1/2"$	72	$2" \times 3^1/2"$
Red 6	4	$3^1/2"$	72	$2" \times 3^1/2"$

Adding Squares to Rectangles
When adding squares to rectangles to make units, use Sally Schneider's "Folded Corners" method.

1. Place a piece of masking tape on your sewing machine straight from the needle toward you. Trim the tape from the feed dogs.

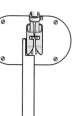

2. Position the pieces to be joined and begin stitching exactly in the corner of the top piece. As you stitch, keep the opposite corner directly on the edge of the masking tape so you can sew a straight line.

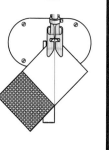

Assembling the Units

To avoid confusion, group the units by number and label each group. After adding each piece to a unit, trim the excess fabric and press.

1. For unit 1, sew a 2" Red 2 square to the left side of a 2" x 3½" tan rectangle as shown; trim. Press the seam toward the red piece. Sew a 2" Red 3 square to the right side of the unit; trim. Press the seam toward the red piece. Make a total of 36 units.

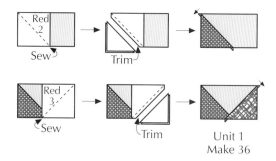

Unit 1
Make 36

2. Refer to the diagram below to sew, trim, and press units 2, 3, and 4. On unit 2, press the seams toward the red pieces; on units 3 and 4, press the seams toward the tan pieces. Make a total of 36 of each unit.

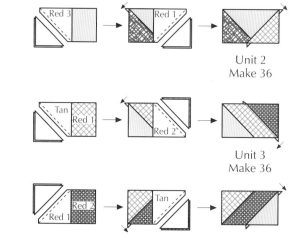

Unit 2
Make 36

Unit 3
Make 36

Unit 4
Make 36

3. For unit 5, sew a 2" x 3½" Red 5 rectangle to the right side of a 2" x 3½" Red 4 rectangle. Press the seam toward the light red piece. Sew a 2" x 3½" Red 6 rectangle to the right side of the unit. Press the seam toward the light red piece. Add a 2" Red 3 square to each end of the unit. Press the seams toward the dark red pieces. Make a total of 72 units.

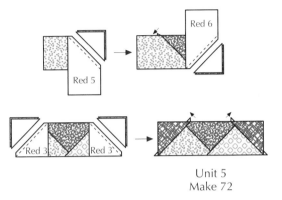

Unit 5
Make 72

4. For unit 6, draw a diagonal line, corner to corner, on each of 36 tan 2⅜" squares. With right sides together, pair each marked square with a Red 3 square. Sew ¼" on each side of the marked line; cut on the marked line. Press the seams toward the dark red pieces. Make a total of 72 units.

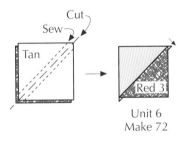

Unit 6
Make 72

Assembling the Rows

1. Row 1 and row 5 are identical. Using 2" tan squares, 2" x 3½" tan rectangles, and units 1 and 2, assemble 36 rows as shown. Press the seams toward the tan pieces.

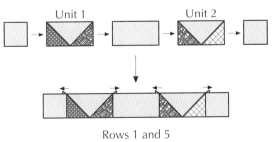

Rows 1 and 5
Make 36

2. Row 2 and row 4 are identical. Using units 3, 4, and 5, assemble 36 rows as shown. Press the seams toward units 3 and 4.

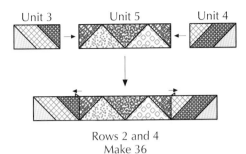

Rows 2 and 4
Make 36

3. Row 3 is used twice in each block. Using a 2" x 3½" tan rectangle and 2 of unit 6, assemble 36 rows as shown. Press the seams toward the tan rectangles.

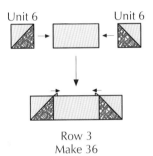

Row 3
Make 36

Assembling the Blocks

1. Arrange the rows, 2 of unit 5, and a 6½" tan square as shown in the diagram below. Sew the rows in the following order:
   Sew row 1 to row 2. Press the seam toward row 1.
   Sew row 4 to row 5. Press the seam toward row 5.
   Sew row 3 to unit 5. Press the seam toward row 3; repeat for an additional unit. Sew these 2 units to opposite sides of the center square. Press the seams toward the square.

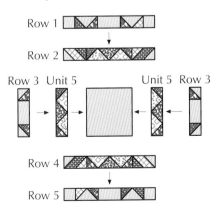

2. Sew the combined top and bottom rows to the center section to complete 1 Cranberry Wreath block. Press the seams toward the outer edges. Make a total of 18 blocks.

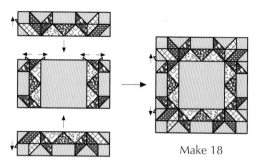

Make 18

Assembling the Quilt Top

Cutting				
First Cut			**Second Cut**	
Fabric	No. Strips	Strip Width	No. Pieces	Dimensions
Background				
Tan	2	14"	5	14" x 14"
	1	10½"	2	10½" x 10½"
Sashing				
Red 5	16	1½"	48	1½" x 12½"
Green	2	1½"	31	1½" x 1½"
Borders				
Tan	7	3½"		
Red 5	7	1½"		

Adding the Sashing and Borders

In sewing the sashing to the blocks, be consistent in the orientation of each block, with rows 1 and 2 always at the top. It's also helpful to sew with the block on top of the sashing strip so you can see the points.

1. Sew 1 sashing strip, 1½" x 12½", to the right side of each block. Press the seam toward the sashing.

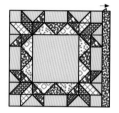

2. Refer to the diagram below to sew additional sashing strips to the blocks and to join the blocks in rows. Make 2 rows of 1 block, 2 rows of 3 blocks, and 2 rows of 5 blocks.

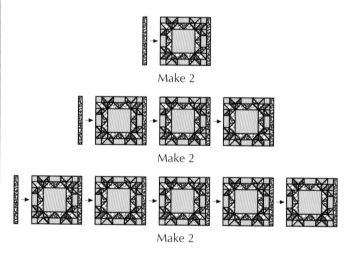

3. Refer to the diagram below to join the 1½" green sashing squares to the remaining 1½" x 12½" sashing strips. Make 2 rows with 1 sashing strip, 2 rows with 3 sashing strips, 2 rows with 5 sashing strips, and 1 row with 6 sashing strips.

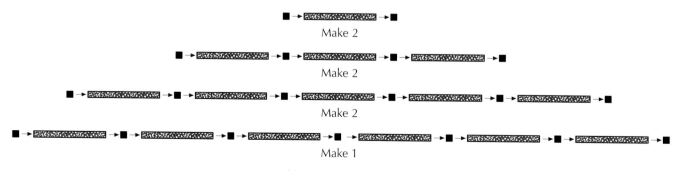

Sashing Strips and Squares

4. Refer to the diagram below to sew the sashing strips assembled in step 3 to the top of each row. Set aside the sashing strip with 6 pieces.

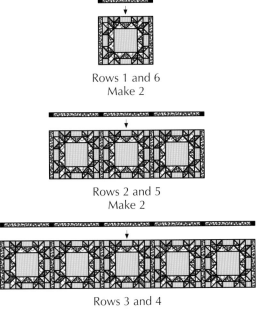

Rows 1 and 6
Make 2

Rows 2 and 5
Make 2

Rows 3 and 4
Make 2

5. Cut the 14" tan squares once diagonally to yield 10 side setting triangles. Cut the 10" tan squares once diagonally to yield 4 corner setting triangles.

6. Arrange the rows, setting triangles, and remaining sashing strip as shown. Join the side setting triangles to the ends of the rows. Press the seams toward the triangles. Join rows 1 and 2, rows 3 and 4 (with the remaining sashing strip in between), and rows 5 and 6; join the sections. Press the seams toward the sashing. Add the corner setting triangles. Press the seams toward the triangles.

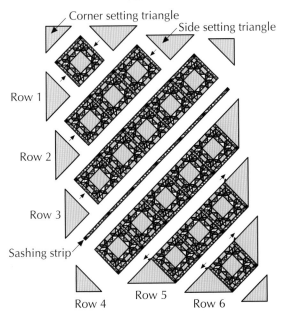

Corner setting triangle
Side setting triangle
Row 1
Row 2
Row 3
Sashing strip
Row 4
Row 5
Row 6

7. Add the inner border, then the outer border, following the directions for "Straight-Cut Borders" on page 13.

Finishing

1. Mark the quilt top as desired or follow the quilting suggestion.

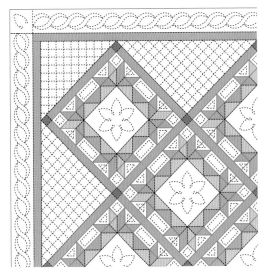

Quilting Suggestion

2. Layer the quilt top with batting and backing; baste.
3. Quilt on the marked lines. (See page 16.)
4. Bind the edges with 2½"-wide Red 5 straight-grain strips. (See pages 17–18.)
5. Sign your quilt. (See page 18.)

Holiday Drunkard's Path

By Vonda Lee Holm

Holiday Drunkard's Path by Vonda Lee Holm, 1993, Monte Vista, Colorado, 32" x 32".

VONDA LEE HOLM

VONDA, A SELF-TAUGHT QUILTER, HAS BEEN DESIGNING AND MAKING QUILTS FOR MORE THAN TWELVE YEARS. SMALL PROJECTS APPEAL TO HER MOST BECAUSE THEY LET HER TRY OUT HER MANY IDEAS AND SEE THE RESULTS QUICKLY.

SEVERAL YEARS AGO, AFTER GROWING TIRED OF STRIP PIECING, VONDA GAVE UP QUILTING—BUT NOT FOR LONG! HER FINGERS WERE EAGER TO STITCH AGAIN, SO SHE TURNED HER CREATIVE ENERGIES TO APPLIQUÉ. SHE SOON DEVELOPED A WAY TO APPLIQUÉ AND QUILT ALL IN ONE STEP, A TECHNIQUE SHE USED TO MAKE HER "HOLIDAY DRUNKARD'S PATH."

VONDA WORKS IN A QUILT SHOP, WHERE SHE TEACHES APPLIQUÉ AS WELL AS TRADITIONAL HAND QUILTING. HER FAVORITE PROJECTS ARE QUILTS SHE DESIGNS AND MAKES FOR SPECIAL FRIENDS BECAUSE, SHE SAYS, "I GET TO THINK OF THEM WITH EVERY STITCH."

TRADITIONAL QUILT PATTERNS, WITH THEIR CLASSIC LINES AND SHAPES, ARE VONDA'S FAVORITES. FOR THE HOLIDAYS, SHE WANTED TO DO SOMETHING DIFFERENT WITH DRUNKARD'S PATH. THIS FESTIVE INTERPRETATION FEATURES GOLD LAMÉ AND A GREEN PRINT WITH GOLD HIGHLIGHTS. METALLIC THREAD AND GOLD BRAID ACCENTUATE THE QUILTING LINES AND CURVILINEAR DESIGN.

Quilt Plan

Quilt Size: 32" x 32"

Materials: 44"-wide fabric

1 yd. muslin for foundation fabric

1 yd. green print for L-shaped pieces and outer border

¾ yd. gold lamé for pie-shaped pieces and inner border

5 yds. flat gold braid, ½" wide

1 yd. for backing

1 yd. thin batting

Metallic thread

Cutting

Use templates on page 97.

From each of the muslin, backing, and batting, cut:
   1 square, 36" x 36".

From the green print, cut:
   4 strips, each 3" x 42", for outer border;
   4 strips, each 3¹/₂" x 42", for L-shaped pieces.
      Stack 2 or 3 strips, right sides up, and cut 44
      of Template A, adding a ¹/₄"-wide seam
      allowance to each piece. You won't need to
      mark the fabric or cut exact seam allowances.

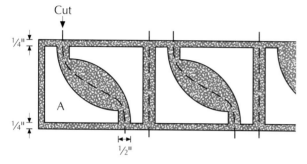

From the gold lamé, cut:
   4 strips, each 2" x 42", for inner border;
   4 strips, each 3¹/₂" x 42", for pie-shaped pieces.
      From each strip, right side up, cut 12 of
      Template B, adding a ¹/₂"-wide seam allow-
      ance to each piece, for a total of 32 B pieces.
      The extra ¹/₄" on the seam allowance allows
      for fraying.

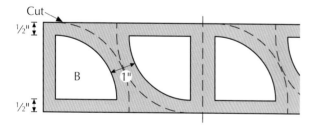

Marking the Foundation Fabric

   To achieve straight borders and near-perfect pieces,
be precise when you mark the foundation fabric.
   1. Fold the 36" muslin square in fourths and finger-
      press the creases.
   2. Lay the muslin square on a flat surface. Mark four

12" squares, using the creases as guides. Then mark
four 6" squares in each of the 12" squares.

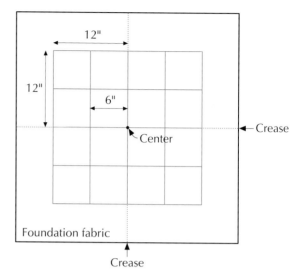

3. Mark four 3" squares in each of the 6" squares, for a
   total of 64 squares. Mark a 1" border for the lamé,
   including the lines for the mitered corners. Mark a
   ¹/₂" border for the foundation fabric; do not mark
   mitered corners. Mark a 2¹/₂" border for the green
   print, including the lines for the mitered corners.

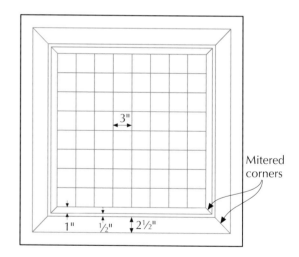

4. Using Template B, mark the curves. Label each piece on the foundation fabric as shown.

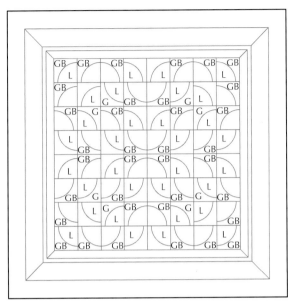

L = Gold lamé
G = Green print
GB = Green print with gold braid

5. Layer the marked foundation fabric with batting and backing. Align the raw edges and pin-baste or baste with thread.

Practicing the "Click" Stitch

With the following method, you use a running stitch to appliqué and quilt at the same time. As with traditional needle-turn appliqué, you turn the raw edge under and stitch the piece to the foundation fabric. However, you stitch through all layers, and the work is done flat, on a magazine. Use large rubber bands to hold the magazine securely on a firm pillow, or tape the magazine to a cardboard box to create a lap work surface.

1. Mark several 3" squares on a piece of muslin. Layer the muslin with the backing and batting; baste. Lay the basted piece, marked side up, on the secured magazine.

2. Keeping the needle at a 45° angle to the flat fabric, push the needle through the layers and into the magazine.

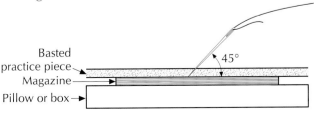

3. Lift the needle out of the magazine—you'll hear a "click"—and bring the needle to the top to complete a stitch. Do 1 stitch at a time, then try taking 2 stitches before pulling the thread to the top.

4. To practice appliquéing pieces, pin or baste a scrap of lamé or green print to the basted piece. (You'll soon learn to appliqué without pinning or basting.) Turn under one edge and, keeping the needle at a 45° angle, place the point on the fold. Stitch as before, going through all layers.

You can also combine the "click" stitch with a traditional appliqué stitch; see page 9. When you pierce the background fabric from the right side, make the stitch "click."

Appliquéing the Pieces

A few guidelines will speed your work and ensure smooth curves and straight edges.

* It's generally best to stitch the curves first, then the straight lines. It's also easiest to begin in the center of the quilt and work out.

* Overlap edges as much as possible. On a straight line where a pie piece and an L piece meet, leave the edges on the pie piece flat. Turn under the edge on the L piece and stitch, overlapping the lamé.

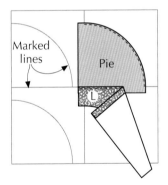

On the inner border, turn under the lamé edges and overlap the L pieces.

* On a curve with braid, stitch the braid as you stitch the curve on the L piece. Check the marked lines on the foundation fabric frequently.

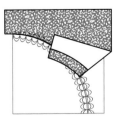

- In a square where the pie and L curves meet, appliqué the pie piece first, then blindstitch the L piece, barely overlapping the curve.

On some squares, such as the corner squares, you will insert braid in this seam.

- Where the braid meets an adjoining piece, leave the straight edge of the piece unstitched so you can slip the end of the braid in the seam. Before you begin, look at the diagram on page 95 to see which edges require this treatment. You can also make the ends of the braid "disappear" by gently bending and slipping them under the seam you're stitching.

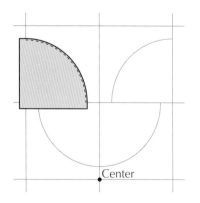

Once you understand the basics, you're ready to begin appliquéing.

1. Thread your needle with metallic thread. Using the marked lines on the foundation fabric as your guide, appliqué the curve on a pie piece near the center of the quilt. (Remember, the lamé pieces have extra-wide seam allowances. You may need to trim them to achieve sharp points.) Repeat for the other pie pieces near the center.

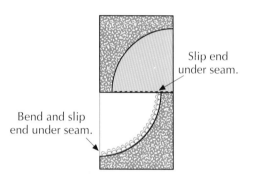

2. Appliqué the L pieces to the center squares, attaching a continuous piece of braid as you stitch the curves. Check the guidelines on the foundation fabric frequently.

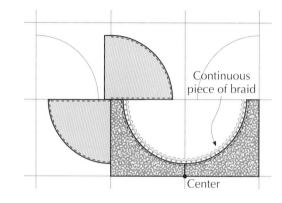

3. Continue adding pie and L pieces and braid, following the diagram on page 95.
4. Add the inner border, turning under the inner edge first, then the mitered corner, then the outer edge. Repeat for the outer border.

Finishing

1. Embellish the green border ½" from the inner edge, using a stem stitch and stitching through all layers.

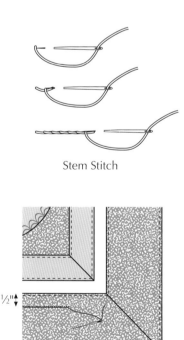

Stem Stitch

2. Quilt as desired or follow the quilting suggestion. On the lamé, use the blunt end of a large needle to make indentations for the quilting lines. On each pie piece, quilt the center line first, then the lines on each side of the center line. Use the "click" stitch or a traditional quilting stitch. Make your stitches a little longer than usual so the metallic thread will sparkle.

Quilting Suggestion

3. With the back of the quilt up, square the edges. Trim the backing and batting (not the foundation fabric) close to the stitching at the outer edge of the border. Bring the foundation fabric to the back and turn it under so the raw edge meets the trimmed edges of the batting and backing. Fold the fabric down and slipstitch to form a self-facing.

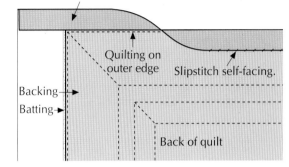

Turn under foundation fabric.

Quilting on outer edge

Slipstitch self-facing.

Backing

Batting

Back of quilt

4. Sign your quilt. (See page 18.)

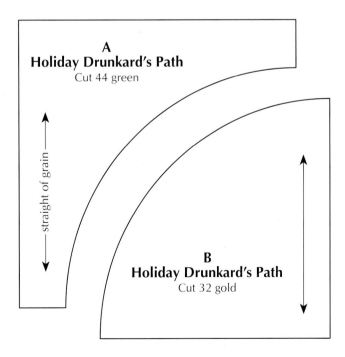

A
Holiday Drunkard's Path
Cut 44 green

straight of grain

B
Holiday Drunkard's Path
Cut 32 gold

Red Ribbons &
Peppermint Candy

By Virda Wilcox Lawrence

Red Ribbons and Peppermint Candy by Virda Wilcox Lawrence, 1994, Lakebay, Washington, 55½" x 55½".

VIRDA WILCOX LAWRENCE

VIRDA WILCOX LAWRENCE OWES HER LOVE OF HANDWORK TO HER MOTHER AND GRANDMOTHER. SHE LEARNED TO EMBROIDER, CROCHET, AND SEW AT HOME. AT THE AGE OF EIGHTEEN, SHE LEARNED TO QUILT AT A CHURCH WOMEN'S AUXILIARY MEETING. SHE SAYS SHE WISHES SOMEONE HAD TOLD HER DURING HIGH SCHOOL GEOMETRY CLASSES THAT THIS WOULD APPLY TO QUILTING; SHE WOULD HAVE PAID MORE ATTENTION!

VIRDA HAS BEEN ACTIVE IN THE QUILTING WORLD SINCE THAT BEGINNING SO LONG AGO. SHE LOVES TO CONTINUALLY INCREASE HER KNOWLEDGE BY ATTENDING AND TEACHING WORKSHOPS. SHE CALLS THE CLASSROOM A "JOINT VENTURE" BECAUSE HER STUDENTS LEARN FROM HER, BUT SHE ALSO LEARNS FROM THEM. IT'S A SHARING EXPERIENCE.

VIRDA LOVES PEOPLE AND SHE LOVES TO QUILT. BESIDES TEACHING FOR SEVERAL LOCAL QUILT SHOPS IN WASHINGTON STATE, VIRDA HAS ALSO TAUGHT IN JAPAN AND ALASKA. SHE IS PAST PRESIDENT OF PORT OR-CHARD QUILTERS' GUILD, NEWSLETTER EDITOR, PAST CHAPTER COORDINATOR FOR THE NATIONAL QUILTING ASSOCIATION, CLOTHING AND TEXTILE ADVISOR FOR PIERCE COUNTY, AND HAS TAUGHT 4-H SUMMER SEWING CLASSES.

VIRDA SAYS THE NAME OF THIS QUILT BRINGS BACK MANY WHIMSICAL, MAGICAL MEMORIES OF HER CHILDHOOD EXPERIENCES—THE SIGHTS, THE SMELLS, THE SOUNDS OF CHRISTMASES PAST. SHE BOUGHT THE STRIPED FABRIC NOT KNOWING WHAT SHE WOULD MAKE WITH IT. SHE NEEDED A NEW CHRISTMAS PROJECT FOR A LOCAL SHOP WHERE SHE TEACHES. VIRDA PUT THE FABRIC ON THE TABLE AND WALKED BY IT SEVERAL TIMES IN THE COURSE OF A DAY. IT HELPED HER START THINKING ABOUT CHRISTMAS—SPECIFICALLY, HOW HER AUNT ILA ALWAYS WRAPPED PRESENTS, WITH A CANDY CANE OR A LITTLE ROLL OF LIFE SAVERS® TIED UP IN THE RED RIBBONS. FUNNY HOW A SIMPLE, HAPPY MEMORY CAN BECOME AN IDEA FOR A QUILT. PERHAPS MAKING IT WILL BRING BACK FOND MEMORIES FOR YOU, TOO.

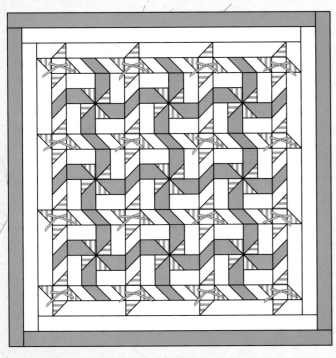

Quilt Plan

Quilt Size: 55½" x 55½"
Finished Block Size: 10" x 10"

Materials: 44"-wide fabric

1 yd. red-and-white stripe for blocks, sashing, and pieced inner border

1¾ yds. red-and-white dot print for blocks, sashing, and outer border

2 yds. white-on-white print for blocks, sashing, pieced inner border, and middle border

3½ yds. for backing

60" x 60" piece of batting

½ yd. red-and-white dot print for binding

8 yds. ⅜"-wide red-and-white polka dot ribbon

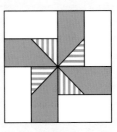

10" Block

Cutting

From the red-and-white stripe, cut:

8 strips, each 3" x 42"; crosscut a total of 100 squares, each 3" x 3", for blocks, sashing, and pieced inner border.

From the red-and-white dot print, cut:

4 strips, each 3" x 53¼", cutting on the lengthwise grain, for outer border;

6 strips, each 3" x 63"; crosscut a total of 60 rectangles, each 3" x 5½", for blocks and sashing.

From the white-on-white print, cut:

4 strips, each 3" x 47¾", cutting on the lengthwise grain, for middle border;

10 strips, each 3" x 72", cutting on the lengthwise grain. From these strips, crosscut:

88 rectangles, each 3" x 5½", for blocks and sashing;

16 squares, each 3" x 3", for sashing;

12 strips, each 3" x 13", for pieced inner border.

Piecing

Blocks and Connectors

1. Use a sharp pencil to draw a diagonal stitching line on the wrong side of each of the 3" x 3" striped squares. Make sure the stripes in each square are oriented in the direction shown before drawing the line. Set aside 16 marked striped squares for the pieced inner border.

2. With right sides together, place a marked striped square at one end of a red rectangle. Pin in place, then stitch on the line. Trim the seam to ¼" and discard the cutaway triangles or set aside for another project. Press the seam toward the striped triangle that remains. Repeat to make a total of 36 units.

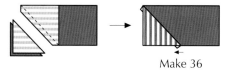

Make 36

3. Sew a 3" x 5½" white rectangle to each of the 36 units and press the seam toward the red rectangle. Make 36.

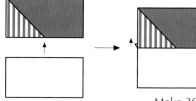

Make 36

4. Arrange 4 of the resulting units as shown. Sew the units together in rows, pressing the seams in opposite directions. Join the rows to complete 1 block. Repeat with the remaining units to make a total of 9 blocks.

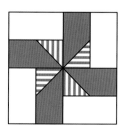

Make 9

5. With right sides together, place a marked striped square on a white rectangle as shown. Pin in place, then stitch on the line. Trim the seam to ¼" and discard the cutaway triangles or set aside for another project. Press the seam toward the striped triangle that remains. Repeat to make a total of 48 units.

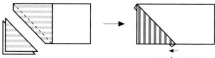

Make 48

Sashing Strips

1. On the wrong side of each of the 48 units made in step 5 above, draw another stitching line at a 45° angle as shown. This line intersects the corner and is 1¾" from the stitching line that joins the striped triangle to the rectangle.

2. With right sides together, place a unit from step 1 on a red 3" x 5½" rectangle. Pin in place. Stitch on the line. Trim the seam to ¼" and discard or set aside the cutaway triangles. Press the seam toward the red. Repeat to make 24 sashing units.

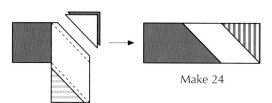

Make 24

3. With right sides together, place a unit made in step 1 on a unit made in step 2. Pin in place, then stitch on the line. Trim the seam to 1/4" and discard or set aside the cutaway triangles. Press the seam toward the red. Repeat this procedure to make a total of 24 completed sashing units.

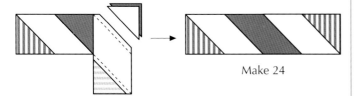

Make 24

4. Make 4 sashing strips, adding 3" x 3" white squares as shown. Press the seams toward the striped fabric. You should have 12 units remaining for the sashing strips between the blocks.

Sashing Strip
Make 4

5. Sew the blocks and the remaining sashing strips together to make 3 identical rows. Press the seams toward the sashing.

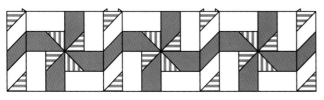

Make 3

6. Sew the rows and sashing strips together as shown, taking care to match all seams.

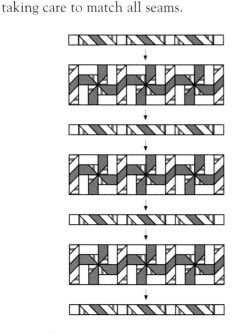

Pieced Inner Border

1. With right sides together, place a marked striped square (set aside earlier) on a 3" x 13" white strip as shown. Pin in place, then stitch on the line. Trim the seam to 1/4" and discard or set aside the cutaway triangles. Press the seam toward the striped triangle. Repeat to make a total of 12 units. Repeat this procedure, using the remaining 4 striped squares and the remaining 3" x 5 1/2" white rectangles.

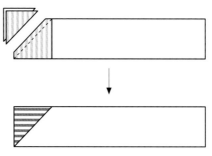

Make 12

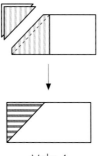

Make 4

2. Make 4 pieced border strips by sewing together the units made in step 1 as shown.

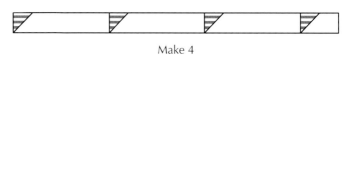

Make 4

Assembling the Quilt Top and Finishing

1. Sew the pieced borders to the quilt top in numerical order as shown. Pin the first border in place, matching seams. Begin stitching strip 1 at the short edge of the striped triangle. Press the seam toward the border strip. Add the remaining border strips, then complete the first seam.

Start stitching here.

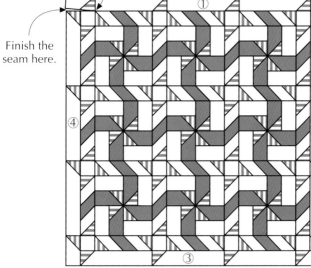

Finish the seam here.

2. Add the 2¹⁄₂" x 47³⁄₄" white border strips in the same manner as you added the pieced border strips. The first border strip should extend 2³⁄₄" beyond the left edge of the quilt. Begin stitching about 2" from the quilt edge. Repeat with the 3" x 53¹⁄₄" red outer border strips.

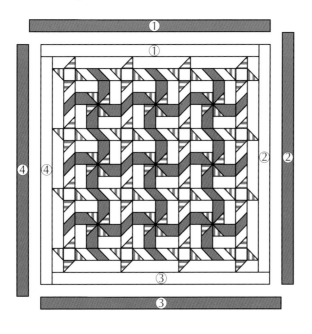

3. Mark the quilt top as desired or follow the quilting suggestion.

Quilting Suggestion

4. Layer the quilt top with batting and backing; baste.
5. Quilt on the marked lines. (See page 16.).
6. Bind the edges with 2¹⁄₂"-wide straight-grain strips of red-and-white dot print. (See pages 17–18.)
7. Cut 16 pieces of the polka dot ribbon, each 18" long. Tie each in a neat bow and cut the ends at an angle. Use small rustproof safety pins to secure a bow to the center of each peppermint candy kiss. Remove ribbons when laundering the quilt.

8. Sign your quilt. (See page 18.)

Chained Stars

By Roxanne Carter

Chained Stars by Roxanne Carter, 1994, Mukilteo, Washington, 70" x 70".

ROXANNE CARTER

ROXANNE CARTER IS A CONSUMMATE QUILTER WHO TEACHES QUILTMAKING PART-TIME FOR LOCAL QUILT SHOPS AND IS A FULL-TIME EMPLOYEE AT THAT PATCHWORK PLACE. SHE HAS BEEN QUILTING FOR THE PAST FOURTEEN YEARS AND IS KNOWN FOR FINDING QUICK AND EASY WAYS TO MAKE QUILTS COME TOGETHER FASTER. AS A TEACHER, SHE IS KNOWN AND LOVED FOR HER PATIENCE AND THOROUGH CLASS PREPARATION AS WELL AS FOR HER OBVIOUS DEDICATION TO HER CRAFT.

ROXANNE CAME UP WITH THIS ORIGI-NAL DESIGN BY COMBINING THE TRADITIONAL LE MOYNE STAR WITH AN INTERLOCKING CHAIN SETTING. SHE DESIGNED IT AS A WAY TO SHOW OFF A COLLECTION OF RAINBOW-COLORED FABRICS, THEN SCALED IT DOWN TO CREATE THIS WONDERFUL CHRISTMAS WALL HANGING. ROXANNE SUGGESTS THAT YOU CONSIDER MAKING THE FOUR RED CHAINS AND THE CENTER CHAIN FROM GOLD LAMÉ FABRIC. THEN YOUR QUILT WILL SYMBOLIZE THE FIVE GOLDEN RINGS THAT WE SING ABOUT IN A FAVORITE CHRISTMAS SONG, "THE TWELVE DAYS OF CHRISTMAS."

Quilt Plan

Quilt Size: 70" x 70"
Finished Block Sizes:
10¼" x 10¼" Star
8" x 8" Snowball
8" x 10¼" Connector

Materials: 44"-wide fabric

3 yds. for block background

1⅝ yds. Christmas print for stars, center chain, and border

1¾ yds. red solid for stars, chains, and binding

1½ yds. green solid for stars, chains, and inner border

4¼ yds. for backing

74" x 74" piece of batting

Star Blocks

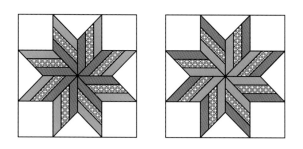

Cutting

From the background fabric, cut:
   3 strips, each 3½" x 42"; crosscut into 36 squares, each 3½" x 3½", for corner squares;
   2 strips, each 5½" x 42"; crosscut into 9 squares, each 5½" x 5½". Cut the squares twice diagonally for side triangles.

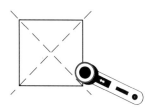

From the Christmas print, cut:
   7 strips, each 1¼" x 42", for stars.
From the red solid, cut:
   7 strips, each 1¼" x 42", for stars.
From the green solid, cut:
   7 strips, each 1¼" x 42", for stars.

Assembly

1. Sew the 1¼"-wide strips together in 7 sets of 3 strips each, with the Christmas print in the center position. Stagger the strips 1" as shown. Press the seams all in one direction.

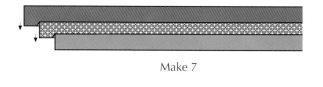

Make 7

2. Using your rotary cutter and ruler, make a 45°-angle cut at the staggered end of each strip-pieced unit. Then cut 2⅝" diamond-shaped segments from the strip-pieced unit. Position the ruler so the 45°-angle line lies along the top edge of the unit. Cut a total of 72 diamonds. You should be able to cut 11 from each unit.

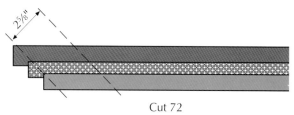

Cut 72

3. Arrange the diamonds and background pieces into a total of 9 blocks, paying careful attention to the color placement for the stripes in the diamonds. You should have 4 stars with green strips meeting in the center and 5 stars with red strips meeting in the center.

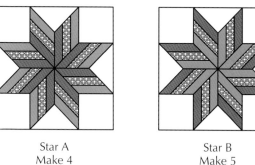

Star A
Make 4

Star B
Make 5

4. Trace the Marking Template (page 109) onto template plastic or heavy card stock. Cut out. Make a small hole where the ¼"-wide seam allowances cross at the tip, sides of the diamond, and one corner. Use this template to mark the seam intersections onto the wrong side of the squares, diamonds, and triangles to make it easy to match the pieces for stitching.

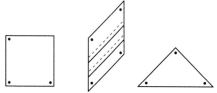

Mark seam intersections.

5. To assemble one block, sew a triangle to each pair of diamonds. To attach the first side of the triangle, begin stitching at the inside point of the triangle and exactly ¼" from the inner edge of the 2 pieces. Stitch all the way to the outer edge of the block, following the direction of the arrow. Sew the second diamond to the triangle in the same manner. Then complete the seam between the 2 diamonds, making sure to match the points. Press the seam to one side and press the triangle seams toward the diamonds.

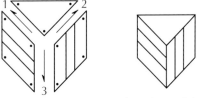

Make 4 for each block.

6. Sew a square to the diamond unit. Start sewing at the outer raw edge of the square and end the stitching ¼" from the inner edge. Sew the second diamond unit to the square. Begin stitching ¼" from the inner point and stitch to the outer edge. Match the points of the diamonds and sew them together; press the seam in one direction. Press the seams between the square and diamond units toward the diamonds. Make 2 half-star units in this manner.

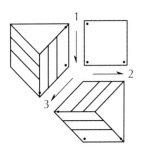

Make 2 for each block.

7. Sew the edges of the diamond units to both edges of 1 square. Stitch from the inner corner to the outer edge of the square. Repeat with the remaining square.

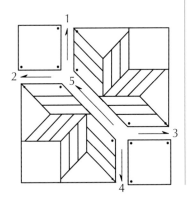

8. Match the center points of the 2 diamond units and pin. Pull the corner squares out of the way and stitch the center seam. Press the center seam to one side; press the seams of the squares toward the diamonds.

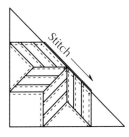

Snowball Blocks

Corner Block   Side Block   Center Block

Cutting
From the red solid, cut:
   16 squares, each 3⅜" x 3⅜".
From the green solid, cut:
   16 squares, each 3⅜" x 3⅜".
From the Christmas print, cut:
   4 squares, each 3⅜" x 3⅜".
From the background fabric, cut:
   16 squares, each 8½" x 8½".

Assembly
1. Draw a diagonal line on the wrong side of each of the small red, green, and Christmas print squares.

2. To make the corner Snowball blocks, place 1 red square face down on the corner of an 8½" square of background fabric, positioning the diagonal line as shown. Stitch on the line and trim ¼" away from the stitching. Press the seam toward the remaining triangle. Make 4.

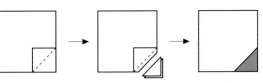

Make 4

3. Make 4 of each color combination shown for the side blocks. Use the same method as described for the corner Snowball blocks. Each side Snowball block has 2 squares attached: 1 red and 1 green.

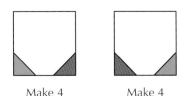

Make 4   Make 4

4. Make 4 center Snowball blocks, following the color placement below. Each center Snowball block has 4 squares attached: 1 red, 2 green, and 1 print.

Make 4

Side Connector Blocks

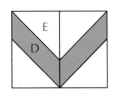

Cutting

From the background fabric, cut:
    24 squares, each 6" x 6". Cut the squares once diagonally for 48 of triangle E.
From the red solid, cut:
    4 strips, each 2½" x 42", for piece D. Cut each strip into 2½" x 10½" segments. You will get 4 from each strip for a total of 16 segments. Place 2 segments wrong sides together and cut a 45° angle on both ends as shown. You will get a mirror image of each piece. Repeat with the remaining red segments.

From the green solid, cut:
    2 strips, each 2½" x 42", for piece D. Cut each strip into 2½" x 10½" segments and then make the angled cuts as shown for the red strips.

Assembly

1. With right sides together, sew the long edge of triangle E to the long edge of red piece D. Repeat on the opposite edge. Make a mirror image of this unit. Press the seams toward the strip in one unit and toward the triangles in the other so that the seams will butt for a perfect match when you sew the units together.

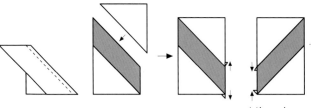

Mirror Image

2. Sew the 2 units together, matching seam intersections carefully. Repeat with the remaining triangles and the red and green D pieces to make 8 red side connector blocks and 4 green side connector blocks.

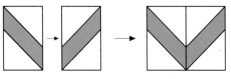

Make 8 red

Make 4 green

Inside Connector Blocks

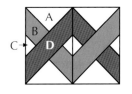

Cutting

From the background fabric, cut:

2 strips, each 6³/₈" x 42"; crosscut into 12 squares, each 6³/₈" x 6³/₈". Cut the squares twice diagonally for 48 of triangle A.

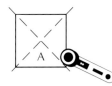

1 strip, 3¹/₂" x 42"; crosscut into 12 squares, each 3¹/₂" x 3¹/₂". Cut the squares twice diagonally as shown above for 48 of triangle C.

From the Christmas print, cut:

1 strip, 2¹/₂" x 42"; crosscut into 4 segments, each 2¹/₂" x 10¹/₂"*;

1 strip, 2¹/₂" x 42"; crosscut into 8 segments, each 2¹/₂" x 4¹/₂"**.

From the red solid, cut:

2 strips, each 2¹/₂" x 42"; crosscut into 8 segments, each 2¹/₂" x 10¹/₂"*;

2 strips, each 2¹/₂" x 42"; crosscut into 24 segments, each 2¹/₂" x 4¹/₂"**.

From the green solid, cut:

3 strips, each 2¹/₂" x 42"; crosscut into 12 segments, each 2¹/₂" x 10¹/₂"*;

3 strips, each 2¹/₂" x 42"; crosscut into 16 segments, each 2¹/₂" x 4¹/₂"**.

*Place all of the 2¹/₂" x 10¹/₂" segments right side up in stacks of no more than 4 and cut a 45° angle at both ends as shown. You should have a total of 24 segments for piece D: 8 red, 12 green, and 4 Christmas print.

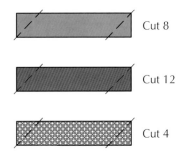

Cut 8

Cut 12

Cut 4

**Place all of the 2¹/₂" x 4¹/₂" segments right side up in stacks of no more than 4 and cut a 45° angle on one end. You should have a total of 48 piece B: 16 red, 24 green, and 8 Christmas print.

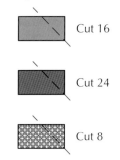

Cut 16

Cut 24

Cut 8

Assembly

1. Sew 1 triangle A to the long side of 1 red piece B. Sew triangle C to the short side of piece B as shown. Press the seams toward the triangles. Repeat with the remaining A and C triangles and B pieces.

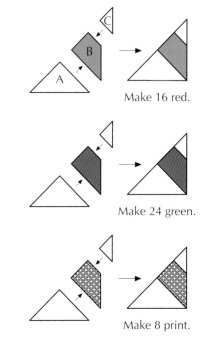

Make 16 red.

Make 24 green.

Make 8 print.

2. Sew 2 matching A/B/C units to the long edges of each piece D as shown, paying careful attention to the color combinations. Press the seams toward piece D in each resulting unit.

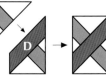

Make 8 Make 8 Make 4 Make 4

3. Make 8 inside connector blocks, sewing a green unit to a red unit as shown.

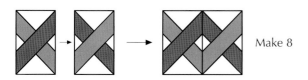

Make 8

4. Make 4 inside connector blocks, sewing a green unit to a Christmas print unit as shown.

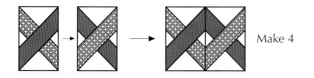

Make 4

Assembling the Quilt Top and Finishing

1. Arrange the blocks in horizontal rows as shown below. Sew the blocks together in rows; press the seams in opposite directions from row to row.

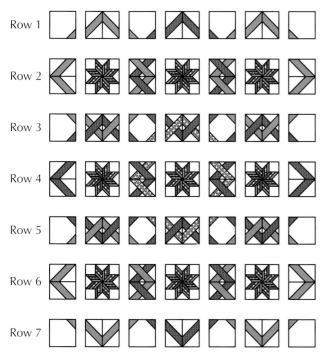

2. Sew the rows together, making sure that the seams match where the connector blocks meet the Snowball blocks.

3. From the green solid, cut 8 strips, each 1½" x 42", for the inner border. Sew the strips together in pairs as shown. Press the seams open.

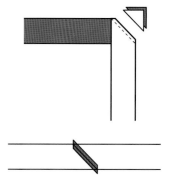

4. From the Christmas print, cut 8 strips, each 4½" x 42", for the outer border. Sew the strips together in pairs as shown above for the inner borders.

5. Sew each inner border strip to an outer border strip and press the seam toward the outer border. Make 4 sets. Trim each border strip to 76" in length.

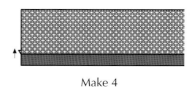

Make 4

6. Sew the pieced borders to the quilt top, following the directions for "Borders with Mitered Corners" on page 14.
7. Mark the quilt top as desired.
8. Layer the quilt top with batting and backing; baste.
9. Quilt on the marked lines. (See page 16.)
10. Bind the edges with your choice of 2½"-wide straight-grain or bias strips of red solid. (See pages 17–18.)
11. Sign your quilt. (See page 18.)

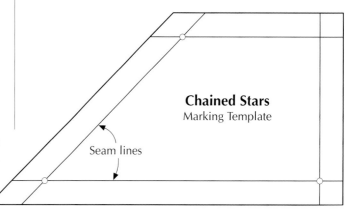

Chained Stars
Marking Template

Seam lines

Snowflake

By Bob Coon

Snowflake by Bob Coon, 1994, Tacoma, Washington, 88″ x 106″.

Bob Coon

Bob comes from a long line of quilters. His mother, Rose Marie, is also a quilter. At the family farm in southwestern Oklahoma, Bob's Grandmother Wald often had a quilt on a frame in front of the picture window for friends to see on their way to town. Bob owns and cherishes several quilts made by his grandmother and great-grandmother.

At the age of twelve, Bob began doing a variety of needle arts. He got his first sewing machine in December 1977, and it has been going ever since.

Bob's teaching career began in Tacoma, Washington, in 1989. Today he teaches at quilt shops in the Northwest and nationally at seminars and quilt guilds. He has developed a reputation for accuracy, creativity, and innovation.

Whether working with traditional designs or creating designs of his own, Bob looks for ways to simplify techniques: "The easier it is for me to do, the easier it will be for my students."

Growing up in Oklahoma, Ohio, and Illinois, Bob experienced the quiet beauty of long, snowy winters. In "Snowflake," he combines crisp white and clear red in a striking Christmas quilt. Bob developed this original design from various traditional patterns, shifting blocks and altering colors until he arrived at a design that possessed simplicity and vitality. You can make this quilt as a queen or twin quilt, or as a wall hanging. To maintain the integrity of the design, Bob designed each quilt with the same number of blocks; only the scale of the blocks varies from quilt to quilt.

Quilt Plan

Quilt Sizes:
88" x 106" Queen
66" x 78" Twin
44" x 52" Crib/Wall

Finished Block Sizes:
12" x 12" Queen
9" x 9" Twin
6" x 6" Crib/Wall

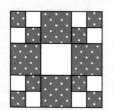

Four Patch/Ninepatch Block

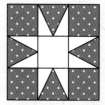

Snowflake Block

Materials: 44"-wide fabric			
	Queen	Twin	Crib/Wall
Red	7½ yds.	4¾ yds.	2½ yds.
White	3¼ yds.	2¼ yds.	1½ yds.
Backing	9½ yds.	5 yds.	3 yds.
Batting	92" x 110"	70" x 82"	48" x 56"
Spiral Binding			
Red	1 yd.	¾ yd.	½ yd.
White	1 yd.	¾ yd.	½ yd.
Note: The quilt in the photo is queen-size.			

Cutting			
Queen			
First Cut		Second Cut	
No. Strips	Strip Width	No. Pieces	Dimensions
Red			
15	2½"	—	2½" x 42"
17	4½"	140	4½" x 4½"
8	4½"	—	4½" x 42"
7	4⅞"	80	Template A
3	20"	5	20" x 20"*
1	12"	2	12" x 12"**
White			
15	2½"	—	2½" x 42"
4	4½"	—	4½" x 42"
3	4½"	20	4½" x 4½"
4	4¾"	80	Template B***
4	4¾"	80	Template Br***

Twin			
First Cut		Second Cut	
No. Strips	Strip Width	No. Pieces	Dimensions
Red			
12	2"	—	2" x 42"
13	3½"	140	3½" x 3½"
6	3½"	—	3½" x 42"
5	3⅞"	80	Template A
3	15"	5	15" x 15"*
1	7½"	2	7½" x 7½"**
White			
12	2"	—	2" x 42"
3	3½"	—	3½" x 42"
2	3½"	20	3½" x 3½"
3	3¾"	80	Template B***
3	3¾"	80	Template Br***

Crib Quilt/Wall Hanging			
First Cut		Second Cut	
No. Strips	Strip Width	No. Pieces	Dimensions
Red			
9	1½"	—	1½" x 42"
10	2½"	140	2½" x 2½"
4	2½"	—	2½" x 42"
4	2⅞"	80	Template A
2	10"	5	10" x 10"*
Scrap	6"	2	6" x 6"**
White			
9	1½"	—	1½" x 42"
2	2½"	—	2½" x 42"
2	2½"	20	2½" x 42"
3	2¾"	80	Template B***
3	2¾"	80	Template Br***

* Cut twice diagonally to yield 20 quarter-square side setting triangles; use 18.

** Cut once diagonally to yield 4 half-square corner triangles.

*** If you fold the strips in half crosswise, you'll automatically cut reversed pieces, such as B and Br, at the same time.

Piecing the Blocks

The instructions that follow are for the queen-size quilt; the measurements in parentheses are for the twin first, then the crib quilt/wall hanging. For example, in step 1, the 2½"-wide strips are for the queen-size quilt, the 2"-wide strips (in parentheses) are for the twin quilt, and the 1½"-wide strips (also in parentheses) are for the crib quilt/wall hanging.

Four Patch/Ninepatch Blocks

Use red thread (or thread to match your darkest color) to piece these blocks.

1. Sew 1 red 2½"-wide strip and 1 white 2½"-wide strip together (2"-wide strips; 1½"-wide strips). Press the seam toward the red strip. Make a total of 15 strip-pieced units (12 units; 9 units). Crosscut each unit into 2½"-wide segments (2"-wide segments, 1½"-wide segments) for a total of 240 segments.

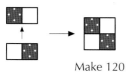

Cut 240

2. Sew the segments together as shown to make 1 Four Patch block. Make a total of 120 Four Patch blocks.

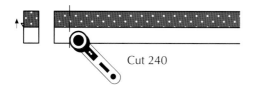

Make 120

3. Sew 1 Four Patch block to each side of 1 red 4½" square (3½" square, 2½" square). Press the seams toward the square. Make a total of 60 units.

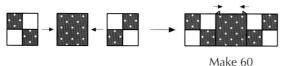

Make 60

4. Sew 1 white 4½"-wide strip between 2 red 4½"-wide strips (3½"-wide strips, 2½"-wide strips). Press the seams toward the red strips. Crosscut the strip-pieced unit into 4½"-wide segments (3½"-wide segments, 2½"-wide segments) for a total of 30 segments.

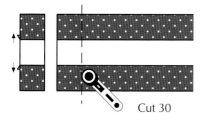

Cut 30

5. Sew 1 four-patch unit to each edge of 1 unit made in step 4 to complete 1 Four Patch/Ninepatch block. Press the seams toward the center unit. Make a total of 30 blocks.

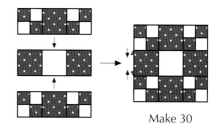

Make 30

Snowflake Blocks

Use the templates on page 115. Use white thread (or thread to match your lightest color) to piece these blocks.

1. Sew 1 white piece B to 1 red piece A as shown. Press the seam toward piece B.

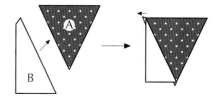

2. Sew 1 white piece Br to the other edge of piece A as shown to make unit 1. Press the seam toward piece Br. Make a total of 80 units.

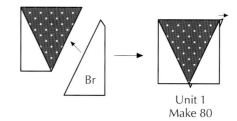

Unit 1
Make 80

3. Sew 1 red 4½" square (3½" square, 2½" square) to each side of unit 1 to make unit 2. Press the seams toward the red squares. Make a total of 40 units.

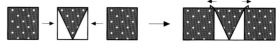

Unit 2
Make 40

4. Sew 2 of unit 1 to each side of 1 white 4½" square (3½" square, 2½" square) to make unit 3. Press the seams toward the square. Make a total of 20 units.

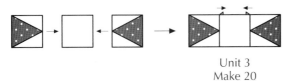

Unit 3
Make 20

5. Sew 2 of unit 2 to 1 of unit 3 to complete the Snow-flake block. Press the seams toward unit 2. Make a total of 20 blocks.

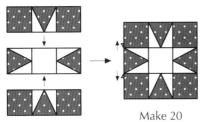

Make 20

Assembling the Quilt Top and Finishing

Use red thread (or thread to match your darkest color) to assemble the quilt top.

1. Arrange the blocks and side setting triangles as shown. Join the blocks and setting triangles in diagonal rows. Press the seams toward the Four Patch/ Ninepatch blocks. Join the rows, making sure to match the block seams. Press the seams in the same direction. Add the corner setting triangles. Press the seams toward the triangles. Because the side and corner setting triangles are oversized, the blocks will appear to "float."

2. Mark the quilt top as desired or follow the quilting suggestion. Trim the quilt corners to round them.

Quilting Suggestion

3. Layer the quilt top with batting and backing; baste.
4. Quilt on the marked lines. (See page 16.)
5. To make the spiral binding, cut 2"-wide crossgrain strips from the red and white binding fabrics. Sew the strips together in sets of 4, alternating red and white and offsetting the strips as shown. On each set, cut a 45° angle at one end, then cut 3½"-wide bias strips from the strip-pieced unit.

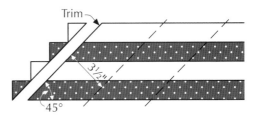

Trim

3½"

45°

6. Sew the pieced strips together to make approximately 11 yds. (8½ yds., 5½ yds.) of binding.
7. Bind the edges with the spiral binding, following the directions in steps 2–9 on pages 17–18, with these important changes: Stitch the binding using a ½"-wide seam allowance. Disregard the references to turning the corners; instead, ease the binding around the curves, being careful not to stretch the binding.
8. Sign your quilt. (See page 18.)

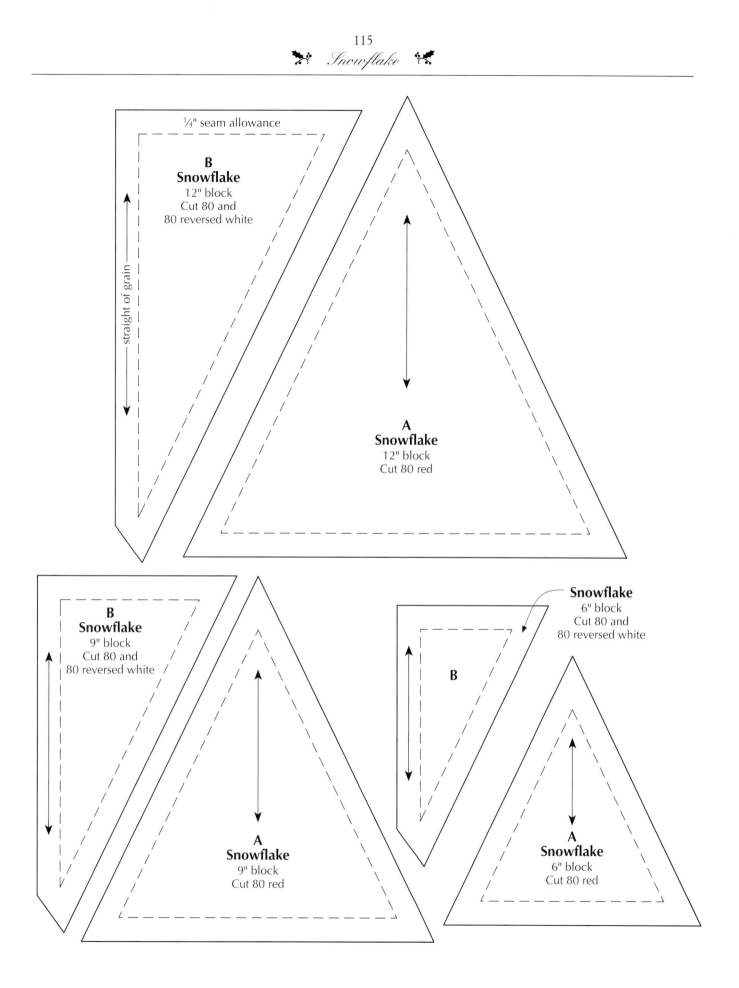

¼" seam allowance

B
Snowflake
12" block
Cut 80 and
80 reversed white

straight of grain

A
Snowflake
12" block
Cut 80 red

B
Snowflake
9" block
Cut 80 and
80 reversed white

A
Snowflake
9" block
Cut 80 red

Snowflake
6" block
Cut 80 and
80 reversed white

B

A
Snowflake
6" block
Cut 80 red

Bountiful Holiday Wreath

By Laura Munson Reinstatler and Joan Dawson

Bountiful Holiday Wreath by Laura Munson Reinstatler, 1994,
Mill Creek, Washington, 34" x 34". Hand appliquéd and machine
quilted by Joan Dawson, Mill Creek, Washington.

LAURA MUNSON REINSTATLER & JOAN DAWSON

LAURA MUNSON REINSTATLER BEGAN HER FIRST QUILT IN 1976—A QUILT THAT TOOK ELEVEN YEARS TO FINISH! SHE BEGAN QUILTING SERIOUSLY IN 1980, DISCOVERING, THROUGH SEMINOLE PIECING, THE POSSIBILITIES FOR EXPLORING COLOR AND VALUE RELATIONSHIPS. FROM SEMINOLE TECHNIQUES, SHE DEVELOPED THE MINI-STRIP PIECING TECHNIQUES THAT BECAME HER SIGNATURE. RECENTLY, LAURA HAS CONCENTRATED HER ENERGIES ON APPLIQUÉ, WHICH SHE AT FIRST COMBINED WITH PIECED WORK.

JOAN DAWSON MADE THIS QUILT USING LAURA'S ORIGINAL DESIGN. LAURA FIRST MET JOAN DAWSON IN 1990, WHEN JOAN TOOK LAURA'S "TWELVE DAYS OF CHRISTMAS" CLASS TO LEARN HOW TO APPLIQUÉ. JOAN DISCOVERED A PASSION FOR APPLIQUÉ, AND SIX OF HER QUILTS WERE INCLUDED IN LAURA'S BOOK *BOTANICAL WREATHS*. THE TWO FRIENDS HAVE A GREAT RELATION-

SHIP: LAURA DESIGNS APPLIQUÉ QUILTS THAT JOAN MAKES, NOW THAT LAURA'S DUTIES AS AN EDITOR FOR THAT PATCHWORK PLACE KEEP HER FROM FULL-TIME QUILTING.

BOTH LAURA AND JOAN LIVE IN THE SEATTLE, WASHINGTON, AREA—LAURA WITH HER HUSBAND, BOB, AND SON, COLIN; AND JOAN WITH HER HUSBAND, AL, AND THEIR FOUR POODLES, LIZA, SARA, BECKY, AND MOLLY.

CELEBRATE THE JOYS OF HOLIDAY GATHERINGS AND LOOK AHEAD TO A PROSPEROUS NEW YEAR WITH THIS FESTIVE WREATH HONORING NATURE'S BOUNTIFUL HARVEST. JOAN USED A HOLLY LEAF AND BERRY FABRIC FOR THE WREATH. APPLIQUÉD APPLES, PEARS, APRICOTS, PLUMS, AND GRAPES COVER A WIDE RIBBON WRAPPED AROUND THE WREATH. CORNER BOWS COMPLETE THIS COLORFUL WALL HANGING.

Quilt Plan

Finished Size: 34" x 34"

Materials: 44"-wide fabric

1½ yds. light tan for background and Border 4

½ yd. red print for corner bows

⅞ yd. leaf print for wreath, Border 3, and binding

⅜ yd. green moiré print for wide ribbon and inner bow loops

¼ yd. red print for ribbon edges and Border 1

¼ yd. purple print for ribbon edges and Borders 2 and 5

Assorted scraps of purples, reds, golds, tans, and browns for fruit and stems

1¼ yds. for backing

36" x 36" piece of batting

Tracing paper or Mylar

Cutting

Use the patterns on pages 120–23
and make appliqué templates, following the
"Basic Appliqué" directions that begin on page 8.

From the light tan background fabric, cut:
    1 square, 23½" x 23½", for the center block;
    4 strips, each 4¼" x 42", for Border 4.

From the red print for bow, cut:
    4 each of ribbon end 32 and 32 reversed;
    4 each of bottom loop 34 and 34 reversed;
    4 each of top loop 36 and 36 reversed;
    4 of knot 37.

From the leaf print, cut:
    5 of wreath piece 1;
    4 strips, each 1½" x 42", for Border 3;
    4 strips, each 1¾" x 42", for binding.

From the green moiré print, cut:
    5 of wide ribbon 6;
    4 each of bottom inner loop 33 and 33 re-
      versed;
    4 each of top inner loop 35 and 35 reversed.

From the red print, cut:
    5 each of narrow ribbon 4 and 5;
    4 strips, each ¾" x 42", for Border 1.

From the purple print, cut:
    5 each of narrow ribbon 2 and 3;
    8 strips, each 1" x 42", for Borders 2 and 5.

From the assorted purple scraps, cut:
    100 grapes;
    10 plums (If you wish, cut a few of these pieces
      from apricot-colored fabric to make apricots
      instead of plums.)

From the red scraps, cut:
    5 apples.

From the gold and tan scraps, cut:
    10 pears.

From the brown scraps, cut:
    30 stems (or you may embroider stems later
      rather than appliquéing them).

Assembling the Center Block

1. To make the wreath pattern, trace the wreath and ribbon sections on pages 120–21 onto tracing paper, tracing 5 of each section in alternating order. Overlap the edges of the sections, matching ribbon edges and dashed lines. (You may use clear Mylar in place of tracing paper. It works well as a placement pattern and lasts longer than tracing paper but cannot be pinned to the fabric easily.)

2. Place the completed wreath tracing over the Ribbon Section with Appliqué templates on page 122 and trace only the fruit on the ribbon sections.

3. Referring to "Basic Appliqué," beginning on page 8, prepare the wreath, ribbon edges, fruit, and stem pieces for appliqué.

Tip:

When you are ready to position each piece for appliqué, place the tracing paper or Mylar pattern over the center of the background square. Carefully slide each prepared piece under the tracing paper and into place.

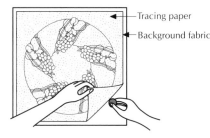

Tracing paper

Background fabric

Place only a few pieces at a time, then pin or baste in place. Appliqué these pieces, then reposition the tracing paper and position additional pieces. Repeat until all pieces are appliquéd.

4. Appliqué all wreath 1 pieces, appliquéing only the inner and outer edges of the wreath sections as shown.

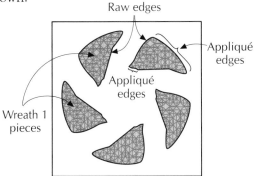

5. Appliqué purple ribbon edges 2 and 3, then red ribbon edges 4 and 5. Appliqué wide green ribbon 6.

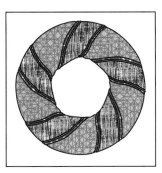

6. Appliqué plum 7, then add grapes 8 and 9 and apple 10. Appliqué grapes 11–21 in numerical order.
7. Appliqué the stem under grape 22, then appliqué grapes 22–28 in numerical order.
8. Appliqué pears 29 and 30, and plum 31.
9. Appliqué or embroider stems on apple, plums, and pears.
10. Trim the center block to 22½" x 22½", making sure that the appliquéd wreath is centered in the square.

Adding the Borders and Corner Bows

1. Measure the quilt top for Border 1 as directed for "Straight-Cut Borders" on page 13 and sew the borders in place. Press the seam allowances toward the borders. Repeat this procedure to add Borders 2 and 3. Add Border 4, following the directions for "Borders with Mitered Corners" on page 14. Add Border 5 as you did Borders 1–3.
2. Referring to the diagram in the next column, appliqué ribbon ends 32 and 32 reversed.

3. Appliqué the remaining pieces of the bow in numerical order.

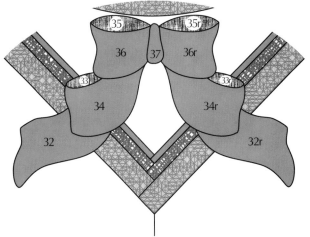

4. Using a contrasting or metallic thread, machine stitch or embroider bow details as shown on the pattern pieces on page 123. Outline the ribbon edges on the wreath with contrasting straight stitching if desired.

Finishing

1. Mark the quilt top. For the center block, Joan quilted a diagonal grid pattern, and she quilted diagonal lines in Border 4. She quilted in-the-ditch around the appliquéd ribbons and bows.

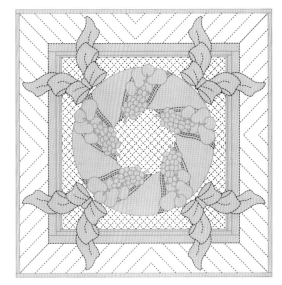

Quilting Suggestion

2. Layer the quilt top with batting and backing; baste.
3. Quilt on the marked lines and in-the-ditch. (See page 16.)
4. Bind the edges with straight-grain strips of the leaf-print fabric. (See pages 17–18.)
5. Sign your quilt. (See page 18.)

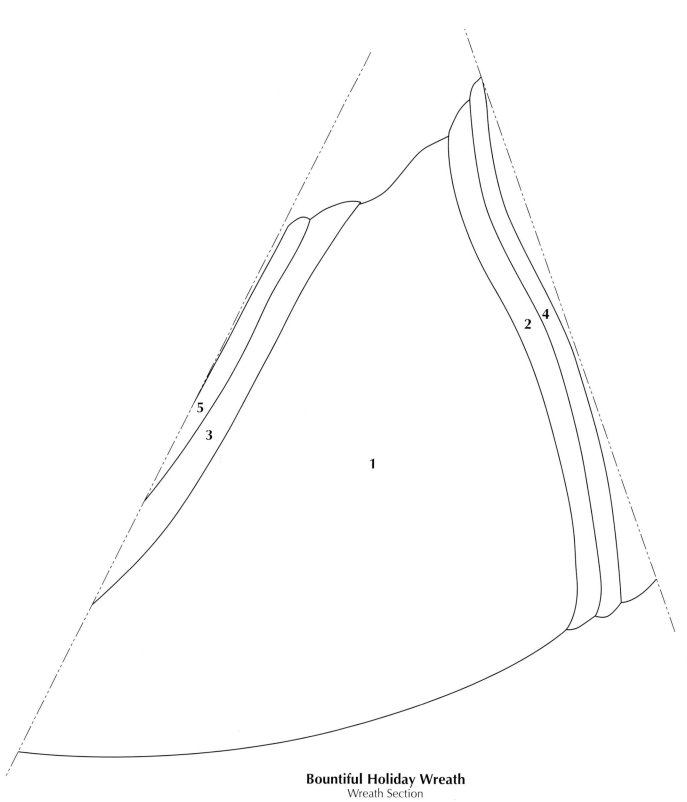

Bountiful Holiday Wreath
Wreath Section

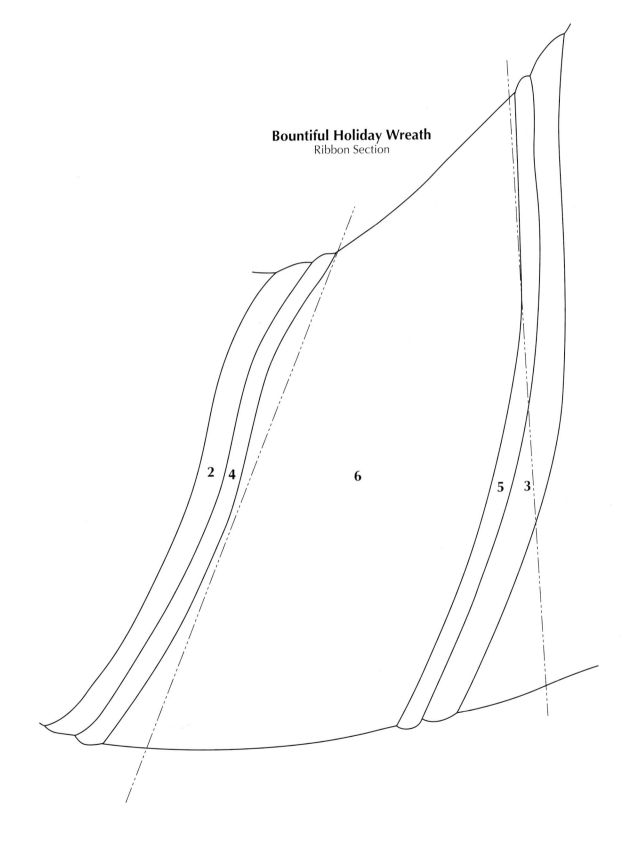

Bountiful Holiday Wreath
Ribbon Section

2 4

6

5 3

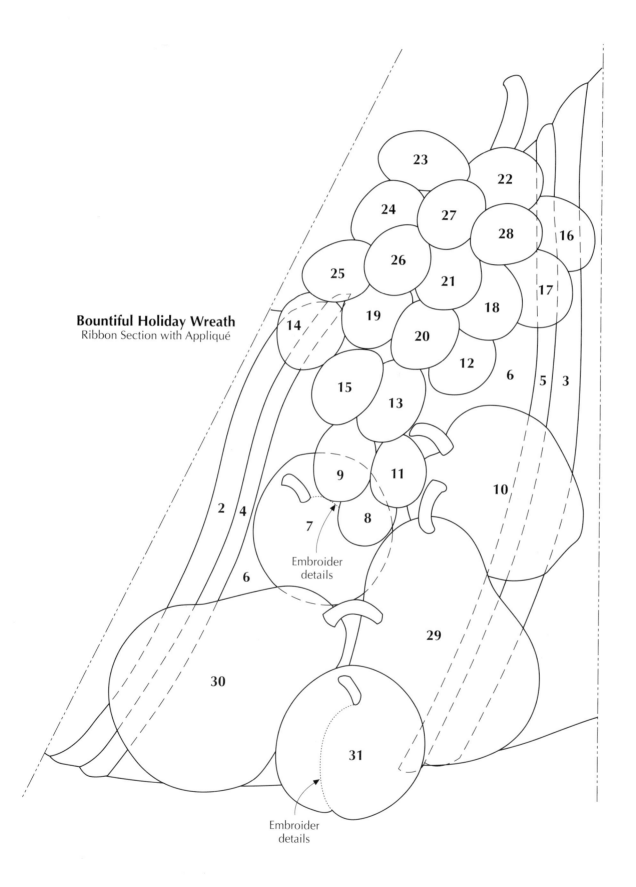

Bountiful Holiday Wreath
Ribbon Section with Appliqué

23

22

24

27

28

16

26

21

18

17

25

19

20

12

6

5

3

15

13

14

9

11

10

7

8

Embroider
details

2 4

6

29

30

31

Embroider
details

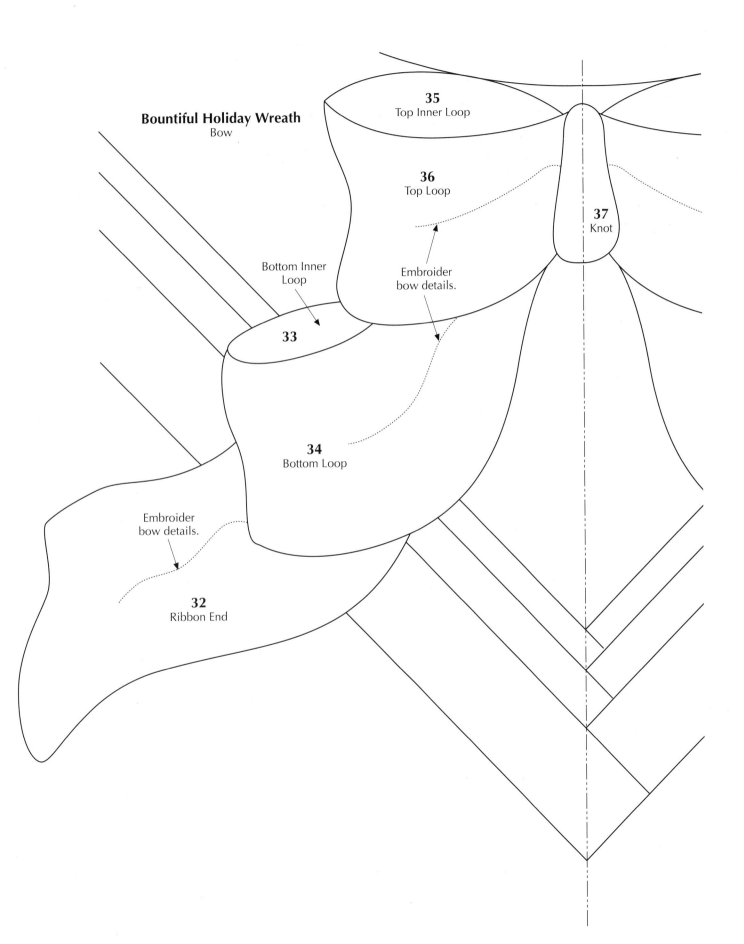

Bountiful Holiday Wreath
Bow

35
Top Inner Loop

36
Top Loop

37
Knot

Bottom Inner
Loop

33

Embroider
bow details.

34
Bottom Loop

Embroider
bow details.

32
Ribbon End

Christmas Morn Tree Skirt

By Gretchen Kluth Hudock

Christmas Morn Tree Skirt by Gretchen Kluth Hudock,
1994, Slinger, Wisconsin, 48" x 48".

GRETCHEN KLUTH HUDOCK

GRETCHEN GRADUATED FROM THE UNIVERSITY OF WISCONSIN—MADISON WITH A DEGREE IN TEXTILES AND CLOTHING AND RELATED ART. HER FIRST QUILT, MADE IN 1976, CONSISTED OF PIECES CUT FROM SCRAPS SHE AND HER SISTERS HAD COLLECTED OVER THE YEARS. GRETCHEN DISCOVERED ROTARY CUTTING IN 1984, AND HER QUILTING CAREER BEGAN IN EARNEST. SHE STARTED DESIGNING QUILTS IN 1989 AND BY 1992 WAS PUBLISHING HER OWN PATTERNS. SHE SAYS THAT HER HUSBAND, RICH, AND HER CHILDREN, JOHN AND ELIZABETH, HELP NAME HER QUILT PATTERNS, AND THE FAMILY DOG OFTEN REARRANGES THE QUILT PIECES BEFORE THEY ARE STITCHED!

GRETCHEN TEACHES A VARIETY OF BEGINNING QUILTING CLASSES. SHE SAYS SHE ENJOYS SEEING BEGINNERS SUCCEED WITH A SMALL PROJECT, GAIN CONFIDENCE, AND MOVE ON TO MORE AMBITIOUS QUILT PATTERNS AND TECHNIQUES.

CHRISTMAS IS GRETCHEN'S SPECIALTY. FESTIVE WALL HANGINGS, TABLE RUNNERS, PILLOWS, AND QUILTED CROSS-STITCH PIECES DECORATE THE HUDOCK HOUSE AT CHRISTMASTIME. AND, OF COURSE, A ONE-OF-A-KIND TREE SKIRT ENCIRCLES THE FAMILY TREE. GRETCHEN'S INSPIRATION FOR HER "CHRISTMAS MORN TREE SKIRT" WAS THE STAR, ALWAYS AN APPROPRIATE THEME FOR HOLIDAY PROJECTS. SHE DESIGNED THE SKIRT USING A COMPUTER PROGRAM FOR QUILTERS, WHICH ALLOWS HER TO MAKE QUICK COLOR AND DESIGN CHANGES. YOU CAN ALSO MAKE HER SIMPLE PATTERN AS A TABLE TOPPER—JUST ELIMINATE THE CENTER HOLE AND STITCH THE OPENING CLOSED.

Skirt Plan

Skirt Size: 48" x 48"

Materials: 44"-wide fabric

Note: This project is not suitable for directional prints.

1 yd. light beige print for background

1 yd. red-and-green holiday print for Four Patch blocks and large triangles

1/3 yd. red print for large triangles

5/8 yd. green print for large triangles

2 yds. for backing

60" bonded, flame-retardant round tree skirt batting* or 54" x 54" piece of batting

* Available from Putnam Co., 810 Wisconsin St., Walworth, WI 53184

Cutting

From the light beige print, cut:

1 strip, 4⅞" x 42", for Four Patch blocks;

1 strip, 4½" x 42"; crosscut into 8 squares, each 4½" x 4½", for Four Patch blocks;

1 strip, 8⅞" x 42", for beige-and-red squares;

2 squares, each 8⅞" x 8⅞", for beige-and-green squares.

From the red-and-green holiday print, cut:

1 strip, 4⅞" x 42", for Four Patch blocks;

1 strip, 8⅞" x 42", for holiday print-and-green squares;

2 squares, each 12½" x 12½"; cut twice diagonally to yield 8 setting triangles.

From the red print, cut:

1 strip, 8⅞" x 42", for beige-and-red squares.

From the green print, cut:

1 strip, 8⅞" x 42", for holiday print-and-green squares;

2 squares, each 8⅞" x 8⅞", for beige-and-green squares.

From the backing, cut:

2 pieces, each 21" x 54";

2 pieces, each 7" x 42".

Piecing the Skirt

1. Layer the 4⅞" x 42" beige strip and the 4⅞" x 42" holiday-print strip, right sides together. Crosscut the strips into 4 squares, each 4⅞" x 4⅞". Cut the squares once diagonally to yield 8 pairs of half-square triangles.

2. Sew 1 pair together diagonally to make 1 pieced square, 4½" x 4½". Carefully press the seam toward the holiday print and trim the "dog-ear" corners. Make a total of 8 pieced beige-and-holiday print squares.

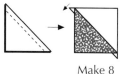

Make 8

3. Sew 1 pieced square and 1 beige square, 4½" x 4½", together as shown to make 1 unit. Press the seam toward the beige square. Make a total of 8 units.

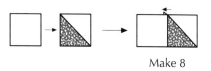

Make 8

4. Sew 2 units together as shown to make 1 Four Patch block. Make a total of 4 Four Patch blocks.

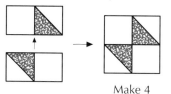

Make 4

5. Arrange the blocks as shown in the piecing diagram below. Sew the left blocks together. Press the seam down. Sew the right blocks together. Press the seam up. Join the top blocks only, stitching from A to B and leaving B to C open. Press the seam to the left.

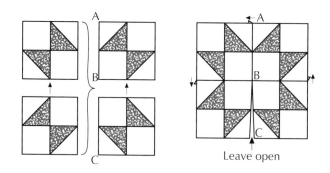

Leave open

6. Layer the 8⅞" x 42" beige strip and the 8⅞" x 42" red strip, right sides together. Crosscut the strips into 4 squares, each 8⅞" x 8⅞". Cut the squares once diagonally to yield 8 pairs of half-square triangles.

7. Sew 1 pair together diagonally to make 1 pieced square, 8½" x 8½". Press the seam toward the red triangle and trim the corners as before. Make a total of 8 pieced beige-and-red squares.

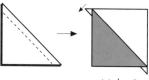

Make 8

8. Layer an 8⅞" beige square and an 8⅞" green square, right sides together. Cut once diagonally to yield 2 pairs of half-square triangles. Repeat with the remaining green square and beige square to yield a total of 4 pairs of half-square triangles. Sew the pairs together to make a total of 4 beige-and-green pieced squares, each 8½" x 8½". Press the seams toward the green triangles.

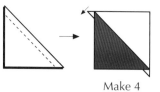

Make 4

9. Layer the 8⅞" x 42" holiday-print strip and the 8⅞" x 42" green strip, right sides together. Crosscut the strips into 4 squares, each 8⅞" x 8⅞". Cut the squares once diagonally to yield 8 pairs of half-square triangles. Sew the pairs together to make a total of 8 holiday print-and-green pieced squares, each 8½" x 8½". Press the seams toward the green triangles.

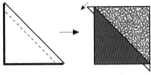

Make 8

10. Sew 2 holiday-print setting triangles to the green edges of a beige-and-green pieced square as shown. Press the seams toward the triangles. Repeat with the remaining triangles and pieced squares to make a total of 4 units.

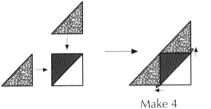

Make 4

11. Sew 2 holiday print-and-green pieced squares together as shown to make 1 unit. Press the seam to the left. Sew 2 beige-and-red pieced squares together to make 1 unit. Press the seam to the right. Sew the units together as shown, matching the seams. Press the seam down. Make a total of 3 units.

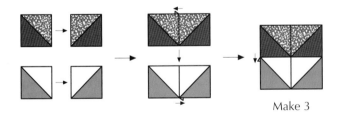

Make 3

12. For the opening, sew 1 beige-and-red pieced square and 1 holiday print-and-green pieced square together as shown to make 1 unit. Press the seam up. Make an additional unit that is the mirror image of the first unit.

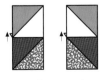

Make 1 each.

Assembling the Skirt and Finishing

1. Arrange the units as shown in the diagram below. Sew the units together in horizontal rows. On the top and bottom rows, press the seams toward the sides; on the middle row, press the seams toward the center. Join the rows, making sure to match the seams. Press the seams away from the center.

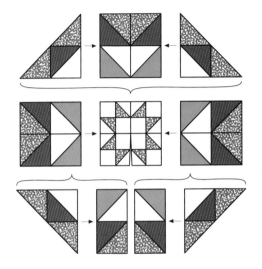

2. Mark the quilt top as desired or follow the quilting suggestion.

Quilting Suggestion

3. Piece the backing as shown, leaving the center seam open from B to C. Press the seams open.

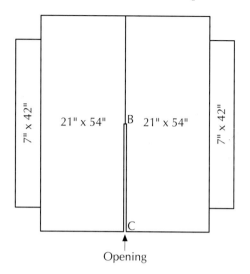

Opening

4. Layer the pieced top and backing, right sides together. Pin. Trim excess backing to within 1" of pieced skirt. Beginning 4" from the center, stitch the left opening edge and around the skirt; stop stitching on the right edge 4" from the center. To keep from losing the points of the triangles, stitch a little closer to the raw edges when you come to intersecting seams.

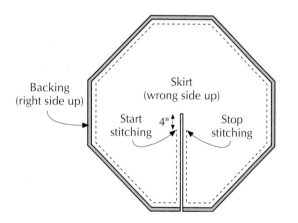

5. Lay the skirt on top of the batting and stitch around the edges again. (Sewing in 2 steps ensures a smooth back on the skirt.) Trim the excess batting and backing even with the raw edges of the pieced top. Trim the corners and points to eliminate bulk. If you're using a piece of regular batting, cut the batting at the skirt opening.

6. Turn the skirt right side out, cutting a little into the center area if necessary. Press the outside edges lightly. Pin-baste the layers.

7. Cut out the center circle. (If you're using a piece of regular batting, mark the center circle using a glass, small bowl, or compass, making the circle smaller for artificial trees and slightly larger for real ones.) Pin the raw edges together. Turn under the unstitched seam allowances on the opening edges and slipstitch.

8. Cut and seam 1½"-wide bias strips of beige fabric to make a length equal to the circumference of the circle plus 16". Find the center of the strip and match it to the point on the circle opposite the opening.

9. Pin the strip to the circle, right sides together, aligning raw edges. Leave an 8" tail at each end. Stitch. Fold the strip to the back and turn under the raw edge to meet the stitching. Slipstitch to the backing. Fold the raw edges of each tail together and slipstitch.

10. Quilt on the marked lines and in-the-ditch. (See page 16.)